ABOUT THE AUTHOR

At the age of eight, Tom Brown, Jr., began to learn tracking and hunting from Stalking Wolf, a displaced Apache Indian. Today Brown is an experienced woodsman whose extraordinary skill has saved many lives, including his own. He manages and teaches one of the largest wilderness and survival schools in the U.S. and has instructed many law enforcement agencies and rescue teams.

Most Berkley Books are available at special quantity discounts for bulk purchases for sales promotions, premiums, fund-raising, or educational use. Special books, or book excerpts, can also be created to fit specific needs.

For details, write: Special Markets, The Berkley Publishing Group, 375 Hudson Street, New York, New York 10014.

GRANDFATHER

TOM BROWN, JR.

BERKLEY BOOKS, NEW YORK

GRANDFATHER

A Berkley Book / published by arrangement with
the author

PRINTING HISTORY
Berkley trade paperback edition / April 1993

Visit our website at
www.penguinputnam.com

ISBN: 0-425-18174-X

BERKLEY®
Berkley Books are published by The Berkley Publishing Group,
a division of Penguin Putnam Inc.,
375 Hudson Street, New York, New York 10014.
BERKLEY and the "B" design
are trademarks belonging to Penguin Putnam Inc.

PRINTED IN THE UNITED STATES OF AMERICA

20   19   18   17   16   15   14

Contents

Introduction

Grandfather was an anachronism. He did not belong in the space and time that I knew him. His wisdom does not fit into modern society but is the call to wilder times and places where all things are real. Modern time and place had no value in his world, for his world was without limits or time. His world was that of nature and eternity. I doubt if he ever really knew how old he was or any of the political boundaries that defined the place of his upbringing. He was truly one of the ancients, part man, part animal, and almost entirely spirit. His home was the wilderness and in wilderness he tested all things. Most of all, he was a searcher of truth, trying to define his world and to preserve the purity. His was a life of grand simplicity that few would ever know, where true riches were defined in beauty and not the false gods of the flesh.

I do not truly know the story of Grandfather's entire life and wanderings. Many things I can only assume. I do know that he wandered throughout his entire life, gathering and preserving the skills of survival, tracking, and awareness, most of all searching for the basic truth in spirit. For instance, he did not just teach me the making of the

1

bow and arrow that was used by his people, but in all, the making of twelve types of bows and arrows. His survival skills come from the far reaches of northern Alaska to the Argentine wilderness, from the East Coast to the West Coast and everything in between. All of the physical skills that he taught were a composition of the various tribes and cultures that spanned the country, selecting the skills that worked for everyone and not the skills that worked for only a few. So too was his knowledge of philosophy and religion, which was even more expansive than his knowledge of practical skills.

Grandfather was born into a small, nomadic clan of Lipan Apaches, sometime in the 1880s, before the Apache people had been fully relocated to the reservations. I can only guess at the specifics of his childhood, about which he was always very vague, from the stories he told. The first two years of his life, until the horror and butchering of war came from the south and killed most of his family and relatives, were spent in the American Southwest. He was then taken south by his great-grandfather, a revered shaman and warrior, to the seclusion of the trackless deserts and mountains. There, with a small group of elders and a few children, he was raised in the old ways. It was a nomadic and simple existence, hidden from the wars that beset the territory and from those who sought to destroy the centuries-old way of the Native American life. The old ones, seeing the greed and destruction that the whites caused, would not permit anything of the outside world to be taught or used by their people. Theirs was a pure existence, of ancient skills and natural wisdom to guide their lives and destiny as a people. When most tribes had fallen prey to the reservations and atrocities of white suppression, Grandfather's people lived free and unfettered. To all but the mountain spirits, it would seem that they did not exist.

Grandfather's people developed the skills of survival, stalking, and tracking to absolute perfection, for these skills were necessary to their survival. In their ability to escape detection they were almost invisible, and the acuity of their awareness kept them safe among the barren rocks and scrub they called home. They deftly moved from one camp to another, living free and wild as their ancestors had. The power of their wisdom, worship, and medicine grew with the ascetic life they lived. The world of the spirit became the single guiding force and the vision of this small group. Their quest was to live in peace, to walk with the Creator, and to keep the old ways alive. It was a life characterized by an extreme simplicity on both a material and a spiritual level. And out of the deepening of an understanding of the spiritual dimension came the ability to speak a different language; the ability to communicate with each other and the natural forces in a real, forceful, and essential way. Grandfather often spoke of his people, of their teachings and love. To this day their legacy remains a guiding force in my life.

It is very difficult to write a book about Grandfather. Not because I do not have enough stories about his life, but rather too many. It is hard to choose those that would fit into any given book. I see now that it would take several books just to cover the most important experiences of his life, and still that would not even come close to covering them all. It became a frustrating task to figure out which stories would fit into this book. Alas, I could only choose those that created his most basic philosophy of wilderness and spirit. There is so much more involved in the fabric of his consciousness, so much detail I was forced to leave out.

An obstacle came to me in the telling of these stories because they are secondhand. I have assumed much in the retelling. The only thing that I feel comfortable with is the fact that when Grandfather told us a story, he didn't just tell it, he relived it, with all the emotion and detail. When he told a story, we too became part of the story and felt much of what he was feeling. The Native American people were such grand storytellers, and I am honored that I have been a student of one of the best storytellers. Still it is so very difficult to retell someone else's life story. No matter how hard I try, there is always the probability of something being left out or not stressed enough.

Another difficulty with retelling a story about Grand-father is that he was locked into the keen perception and sensitivity to the world of nature and spirit. I'm sure that no matter how much he relived a story, he had to have left so much of the experience out. I'm reminded of his incredible observation powers almost on a daily basis. For most people, a short walk in the woods was just that, but to Grandfather it was an experience rich with natural wonders and spiritual rapture. We couldn't walk ten feet together without Grandfather pointing out to me countless things that I had missed on a physical level. The things I used to miss on a spiritual level were even more exasperating. This leaves me to often wonder about those many things that Grandfather left unmentioned in his stories. Without those things I feel that I cannot do his experience justice.

The writing of this book has been one of my most difficult tasks. It is not just the countless hours going through my dusty old journals that help jog my memory. And it isn't the fact that I had to return so often to the place in the Pine Barrens, New Jersey, where the stories were once told. It is mostly the fact that I feel guilty. Guilty for attempting to tell his story and guilty because I know that I cannot do it justice. So too is the guilt about making the wrong choices for the stories included in this book. All I can do is rely on what my heart tells me to do and then do the best I can.

Many readers and students ask me why I now choose to write a book about some of Grandfather's life. After fourteen years of teaching and twelve books, I feel that it will answer many of the questions as to where the philosophy and the skills that I teach originated. Grandfather, after all, was one of the biggest influences in my life and how he learned his skills is more important than how they were passed on to me. His skills and philosophy were not strictly of the Native American culture, but a result of his wanderings and searching. For me it was important to know how he arrived at the conclusions he did, and the circumstances and teachers surrounding this enlightenment.

My books, *The Tracker, The Search*, and *The Vision*, have dealt with some of my life story. The numerous field guides on tracking, survival, and awareness deal with the various skills needed to take someone back to the wilderness and become, once again, a child of the earth. *The Quest* and *The Journey* deal primarily with the philosophy of wilderness and the deeper spiritual quests. Finally, *Grandfather* brings this all together as it lightly touches some of the origins of these teachings. It will give my readers and students alike a greater understanding of who this man Stalking Wolf was and the ultimate impact he had on my life and on so many others.

1

Grandfather's Quest

As I see it, Grandfather had just three missions in his life. His first mission was to try to learn, preserve, and pass down as many of the old skills of survival, tracking, and awareness as possible, and do so by living with the earth with as little as he could. It was not just the practical and physical skills of his people that were important to him, but of all peoples that lived close to the earth. He sought out anyone with any primitive skill, no matter if it came from the Native American culture or some old hermit living in the bush; everything interested him and he wanted to learn everything. His quest to try to find and learn these skills took him from Alaska to South America, from the East Coast to the West Coast of America, and everywhere in between. He wanted to learn skills that could be used in any environment, any weather condition, and in any topography. Most of all, he wanted to know what skills would become universal to all places and situations. So too he would learn the skills known both by the men and by the women.

Grandfather could see that these ancient skills were being lost to modern man. To him, they were the doorway back to

5

the earth and the ultimate freedom from society's strangling grip. They were a way to fulfill one's purpose for being born to the earth; to make things better for future generations by caretaking creation. The survival skills were a tool that would end the struggle between man and nature, where there was no longer any clash, only a perfect balance and harmony. It is through these skills that man can make a home in wilderness, a real Garden of Eden, where all struggle was finally ended. So the preservation and use of these skills became his first quest, a quest that would not end until the day he took his final walk.

His second quest in life was to preserve the ancient spiritual wisdom, not only of his people, but anyone who lived close to the earth. He did not seek the things that did not work, or worked only for a few, but he sought a truth that produced miraculous results. He was determined to find, preserve, and pass down spiritual wisdom that was viable and would work all of the time. He sought a dynamic communication with the world of nature and the realm of spirit that would work for anyone and everyone. He knew that living in nature on a physical level was but a small part of the whole consciousness of wilderness. Man had to go deeper than just the flesh, otherwise man's existence in the world of nature would still contain a deep separation. Without spiritual skills, man could not become "one" with the natural world, nor communicate with the things beyond flesh.

His final quest was to learn all that he could from every philosophy and religion. He sought a common truth, free from the crutches of man. He searched through all the customs, the ceremonies, the dogmas, and the traditions of religion and philosophy, stripping away all the confusing camouflage and arriving at a "pure truth." It was the search for these spiritual truths and spiritual knowledge that was the main driving force in his life. In all that he pursued, the spiritual was the foremost on his mind. Even when he taught Rick and me, most of what he passed down was that of the spirit. Even the practical skills had deeper spiritual meaning, so that there was rarely a time or a lesson that did not encompass his spiritual teachings.

Grandfather's quest, his search for the "truth," led him far from his people and from a life that would be considered normal by any standards. He abandoned his people and lay down his life for his quest. For sixty-three years of his life he wandered and searched, many times living on the edge of life and death. So too did he face many hardships that would have driven most men from their paths. He pushed himself hard, never being satisfied with just a superficial understanding, but instead seeking the deeper and more profound meanings of skill and spirit. He drove himself harder than anyone I have yet encountered in life and I long to be able to have the resolve and dedication that he had. Nothing distracted him from that path, not even the hopelessness of his overall vision: the vision to try to save the earth by teaching the truth. Even when no one would listen, he would not give up, for there was always hope and he had to live his vision or not live at all.

It was within the first few months of our meeting that Grandfather told us what had driven him to this quest. We had been curious as to what had led him to this path and it was only after a lot of coaxing and prodding that he revealed his story to us. It was the story of the white coyote and the spirit warrior that would forever change his path. That one night, sitting by a small campfire deep in the heart of the Pine Barrens, Grandfather revealed to us the vision that drove him to his path. The reason that he faced so much hardship and endless lonely searching. A quest that he had to undertake without question.

Grandfather began his life, as all small children did, learning the ways of gathering herbs, cooking, mending, and making camp, as well as learning the philosophy and mythology behind each activity and skill. All things "of the camp" were of the domain of the women of the tribe, and it was in these matters that Grandfather was first schooled. These teachings were never thought of as being lesser but rather as necessary life skills for the hunter and scout. To his people, within their vision of the completeness of life, innate power or spiritual growth existed regardless of gender. All skills were necessary to keep the camp alive. So Grandfather was taught all the things of the camp. From the women, he learned the compassion of healing, the mothering instinct, and the profound patience that would serve him throughout his life. The women of his people were always highly respected for their power and medicine. It was the women who gave him his first spiritual tutoring, which was the catalyst that started him on his spiritual path.

Grandfather was the youngest member of the small group of displaced Apaches and as such was somewhat of a child to all. But his great-grandfather, Coyote Thunder, was his foremost guardian and his most powerful teacher. Even while Grandfather was under the tutelage of the women of the tribe, Coyote Thunder still oversaw his education.

By tradition, Grandfather was, at age seven, officially given over to the care and teaching of Coyote Thunder and the other tribesmen, in order to learn the ways of the men. Now he began to learn the skills of the hunt. He learned to make bows, lances, clubs, arrowheads, and traps. As with the lessons of the camp, each lesson of the hunt—each new tool, each new skill—was accompanied by a story explaining the underlying spiritual implication. Later he learned to trap and track; he learned the honor of the hunt and the dignity of stalking. It was from his prowess as a stalker that Grandfather acquired the name Stalking Wolf. One day some of the elders watched him stalk and then touch a wolf—one of the most aware, cunning, and hence most difficult of animals to catch. Thus, in ceremony, Grandfather was renamed.

Stalking Wolf became one of the greatest hunters of the group, always providing meat as well as medicinal herbs. Always, when returning from a hunt, he would first feed the sick and weak or bring them the medicinal herbs he had collected from his hunting trip. By the time he had reached ten winters, he was leading his own hunting parties. But Grandfather preferred to hunt alone, and it was on such a hunt that he was given a vision, a powerful vision that would change his life and direct him toward a path of medicine. Certainly before he had undertaken ritual quests of the spirit, and with each quest he had gained insight and understanding. But the grand visions of life come infrequently, and then only after long searching and many vision quests. This, however, was the first vision to address the questions of his path and purpose in life, a guiding force that would prepare the ground for future visions and quests.

He was hunting alone, far from his people. This hunt was for the mountain lion, an animal whose stealth awareness almost always required the hunter to be alone. He had been fasting for the entire hunt—four days in all—and had traveled without rest to the place where his father had once killed a white mountain lion, the skin of which Grandfather still used for his medicine bundle. Upon reaching his destination, he climbed a high ridge to sit and pray. A spirit in the guise of an ancient warrior and scout appeared before him. The spirit just stood there, looking at him. It was a searching look, searing through his flesh, looking straight through to Grandfather's heart and spirit. When Grandfather tried to communicate with the spirit, using both language and sign, he was ignored. And so, for a long time, they each stared at the other. Grandfather said that he was at once both fascinated and fearful. Instinctively, however, he knew that the ancient one was a messenger from the bright vision, not from darkness.

The spirit then approached Grandfather. In his right hand he held the ancient headband of the scout society and in his left hand he held the feathered staff of the shaman. Without word or ceremony he first handed Grandfather the scout headband, paused, then handed him the staff. Grandfather trembled inwardly with fear and excitement, unable to think or move. The spirit backed away and resumed his silent vigil, gazing at Grandfather as he held the gifts in his outstretched hands. Slowly, feeling the powerful force of the medicine items he held, Grandfather drew them in and clutched them to his chest. His motion was the symbol of accepted gift and spiritual possession. At this sign of acceptance the ancient one smiled, nodding slightly, then made the sign for ten winters, ten years, and faded from view. In his place stood a huge white mountain lion. It growled at the sky, turned, and then slipped from white to gray and then to shadow.

Grandfather was shaken with what he had just experienced. The objects he held were very old and tattered but they were very real and extraordinarily beautiful. He was aware of the awesome power, the mystery, they contained, and the honor of holding them. They were fascinating, compelling, as if containing the knowledge of the ages. He sat until dark, rethinking what he had witnessed, and the mystery of all that had happened overwhelmed him. He had so many questions, and the answers that came were vague at best.

He arose from this place and walked down to the creek to wash. From the mists of dusk, the spirit reappeared, this time accompanied by the white mountain lion walking by his side. From across the creek, the spirit again stood facing him, watching. Again, after a long oppressive silence, he made the sign for sixty winters and gestured toward Grandfather. The mountain lion arose and leapt across the creek to Grandfather. With an uttered sound the lion passed to Grandfather the ancient medicine of the traveler, while across the riverbank the ancient one pointed the directions. Motioning to the east, the spirit and the lion faded into the shadows. Grandfather looked toward the eastern horizon where the spirit had last pointed, and there, in a cluster of pines, stood a young white coyote. But it too faded from view, vanishing into the moonlight. Grandfather was even more shaken. Greater questions fell around him. Try as he might nothing seemed to make any sense.

Grandfather stayed in this sacred place for four more days, waiting for explanations, searching for answers. Perhaps there would be yet another vision, one that would dispel his confusion. When earth and spirit refused to speak, however, he headed back to the tribe, and to the wisdom of the elders. The ancient tradition was to seek out the guidance of the elders and tribal shamans, especially where a vision was concerned. The elders had always helped before, on all his quests and spiritual searchings, but he wondered if they could really help him now. He didn't even know if he should reveal any of what he had seen or, for that matter, show them the sacred staff and headband. Did his reluctance to share these matters stem simply from a feeling of possessiveness or could it possibly be that in the sharing he would be violating some sacred trust between himself and the spirit of the scout? He took his time with the journey back to the encampment so he would have plenty of time to search his heart for answers.

By the time camp came into view, he knew what he would have to do, and that was to ask the elders to help. He had searched his heart for this answer and it felt good; his heart was, he knew, the only thing he could truly trust for clear thinking. And so he asked the elders to give him a council fire, following the old tradition of presenting them all with gifts for their time, effort, and wisdom. That night, in a

simple ceremony, Grandfather danced his vision, describing
in detail its events and symbols. He displayed the sacred
items, but sensing the sacredness and power within, none
would touch or disturb them. Once the vision story was
complete, the elders asked Grandfather a few questions for
clarity, then sent him away. It was customary to leave the
elders in silence, once the vision was told. This would give
the elders time to discuss the vision, and the seeker time
to meditate. It would also allow the elders time to prepare
for any ceremony or ordeal that they felt the seeker should
witness.

Four days later, Grandfather was called from the hills, his
personal place of solitude and prayer, to sit before the elders.
They met him in a big brushy lodge at the far edge of camp.
The mood was somber and reverent. They sat in a semicircle
before a small fire and the smoke of many sacred herbs hung
heavy in the rafters. Opposite the semicircle, Grandfather
sat alone before the fire, awaiting patiently the reply of the
elders. Coyote Thunder spoke first, his voice weak with age,
trembling with sadness. Yet the gleam in his eye held hope
and pride. He told Grandfather that the vision and the spirit
had guided him toward a path he must take. To follow his
vision he must first spend ten winters training to become
a scout, one of the most powerful positions in the tribe.
He must then abandon this path for another ten winters
and seek the path of a shaman and healer. And finally,
Coyote told him, he would have to leave his people and
wander alone for sixty more winters, seeking vision and
knowledge, until his vision was reality.

Grandfather's spirit soared at the thought of becoming a
scout and he felt greatly honored that he had been chosen for
the path of the shaman. But his heart was sad at the prospect
of having to leave his people and his homeland for so long
a time. He asked Coyote if there was a way he could stay
and still fulfill his vision, a way in which all could share
with him his honor and he could honor his people. Coyote
was adamant in his refusal. "A man not living his vision is
living death. Unless there is a question that the vision was
a trick of the mind, the vision should never be altered. But
the sacred items I hold are real, and so the vision is real."

Coyote went on to explain that Grandfather's calling
was from the Creator and its undertaking was necessary

for the overall vision of his people and of the earth: that although Coyote's heart would be sick and sad at Grandfather's eventual departure, the journey was essential, even critical. Coyote ended by saying, "You have been my hope for many years, my life, but at the end of the training, for the good of all things you must go." The other elders, men and women, echoed the feelings of Coyote and encouraged Grandfather in his quest. There was no communal ceremony or feast at the finish of this council, for Grandfather had chosen the life of the scout, a path that would, throughout his training, separate him from the group. With this exile he would begin his journey. He would now sleep alone, eat alone, and live alone.

Grandfather then journeyed frequently, for weeks at a stretch and without any man-made tools, into the harshest lands. He honed his survival skills until they became instinctual. He came to look upon even the most violent and lonely of places as home, and found comfort and security where other men would only find death. He became an animal again, a shadow living on pure sunshine and air. Survival and the ability to face any environment without the need of any supplies were skills essential to the scout. Thus, the many skills of survival and the philosophy behind them became Grandfather's first priority. It was only through survival that a scout learned to become one with the landscape, to find refuge in the most rugged terrains.

Survival practice took Grandfather far from his people for great periods of time and introduced him to many landscapes and environments. He learned how to survive easily in the hottest deserts, on the mesas, on the plains, in the coldest snows, and in the depths of the deepest forests. Each survival test the elders put him through he easily passed, oftentimes to the disbelief of the old ones. Where he should have been emaciated with starvation and exposure, he seemed to flourish. He could live where no one else could; he could travel at great speeds and over great distances where even the animals faltered. His skill was unparalleled by any tribal member and even the noted elders marveled at his ability.

Once the survival skills were mastered, he was then led to the arts of tracking, stalking, and awareness. Absolute proficiency in these skills—the ability to move, silent and unseen, across landscapes with little cover, the ability to observe all things at a glance—were essential to a scout. Tracking, stalking, and awareness are never separated but rather viewed as a whole, a sort of continuum in which one is dependent on the others for absolute precision and perfection. These skills, coupled with the ability to survive, made of the scout a shadowy ghost, mystical and shrouded in an air of secrecy and legend, much like the ancient ninjas. Grandfather's lessons and ordeal were soon intensified in these areas. The tests of the elders pushed Grandfather to the limits of his ability and beyond.

Grandfather worked long and hard, pushing himself harder than the elders pushed him, always holding his vision as a driving force, always trying to live up to and beyond the expectations of the elders. He stalked without ceasing, slipping unobserved in and out of camp. He tracked, stalked, and ultimately touched all manner of animals, moving as if composed more of spirit than of flesh. He added danger to his tests by stalking powerful animals, where one mistake could cost him his life. Finally he stalked and tracked the camps of others: hostile tribes, cavalry, and settlers. He pushed his skill to the limits of mortal man, traveling along open ground, never observed in form or in track by his enemies. Truly he lived up to his name as the one who stalks wolves.

It was awareness lessons and tests, however, that were of paramount importance. For Grandfather, for the scout, awareness of all things, close and afar, was essential both to his own personal survival and to the survival of his people. It was the scout's awareness that kept his people safe. So Stalking Wolf pushed himself to observe at all levels, not only on the physical level but also on a deeper, more encompassing, spiritual level. Eventually his skills transcended the mere senses, and he began to reach beyond to the force of life itself. The confluence of physical sensing and spiritual awareness was eventually so complete that when asked how he knew that something was moving in the distance, he was often at a loss to explain. Complete awareness became for him a state of being. It was said of him that if a feather dropped from a bird several miles away, Grandfather would know about it. This keen awareness, surely and inexorably, began to break down the distinction between the inner and outer dimensions, creating a oneness of the self, where nothing happened that he could not feel.

Then came the training that Grandfather hated but had to learn—the kill. The mark of a good scout was the ability to become invisible, to be able to get in and get out of situations without being detected, but sometimes his life depended on his fighting ability. Grandfather abhorred warfare and the pain and slaughter that went with it, but he learned its skills just as well as he had those of absolute survival, tracking, stalking, and observation. He understood the necessity of the fight, but his heart would never agree with his ability, nor could he find any honor in it, and so during the tests of the fight and the kill he would never hurt an enemy, only take their weapons, tie them up, or mark part of their flesh in red to show how the kill would have taken place. Only a few times did he have to fight, but these fights ended quickly because of his agility and the strength acquired from his powerful life-style.

Sometimes Grandfather would lead bands of warriors to distant lands to check on neighbors to ensure the security of his tribe. Only once did he actually have to fight and that was when he rescued a young Lipan woman from her captors. He left them alive, unharmed, and ashamed. He became a powerful force among his people, an excellent scout, and though he was very young, he was considered by many to be an elder, or Grandfather, meaning teacher. To nearby tribes and cavalry his prowess assumed mythic proportions. He was so feared by many that even a fleeting appearance by him at the edge of camp would send warriors into blind panic. To neighboring tribes every time something went wrong or was missing, the people would smile and blame it on Grandfather. When someone was walking alone and felt he was being watched, the common expression was that the "wolf" was doing the watching, or he was "wolf-watched," as it was sometimes called.

As Grandfather's skill as a scout neared perfection, the elders held a council with him again. It was just past five winters from the first major meeting, and they met as they had before, in the big lodge at the edge of the old village. Again he faced the elders but this time the ambience of the lodge and the mood of the old ones were different. The lodge itself had remained the same—the fire at its center was low, and the smoky scents of sacred herbs hung in the air. Now,

however, the lodge was filled with the myriad sacred items
of the tribe and the elders wore their most sacred attire. The
attitude was one of reverential worship. A lone drum rang
out softly from the dark recesses of the outer lodge poles,
and there was a presence beyond that of the elders. It was
a powerful feeling, a feeling that the spirit world stood with
rapt attention, watching, waiting, guiding the words that the
elders would speak. The old ones seemed to be listening,
beyond the mortal sounds of the night, to voices that only
the pure heart could hear.

Grandfather stayed in the lodge for six days of teaching from the elders. They all fasted; they all prayed. Sleep
was rare. When one elder counseled Grandfather, the others would sleep. His mind and emotion, body and spirit,
swooned with fatigue and the intensity of it all, but he held
on. He knew that this was his initiation to an apprenticeship
in the shamanic way of life. This had been his vision. This
was his driving force, and he wanted to live this vision or
not live at all.

The lessons imparted during this session in the lodge
formed the essentials of a code of ethics by which the healer
and shaman lived, a direction, and a path to greater spiritual power. Chant, song, and ceremony followed each of
the major lessons. At these times the lodge would come
alive with sound and motion, freeing Grandfather's spirit
from the talons of fatigue. At the end of the sixth day
Grandfather was sent away for his first test—he would wander the deserts for two moons. At the end of this time he
would return to the elders, if he was still alive, for further
counsel.

The desert felt like a furnace. His task was to face this
emptiness purely, to live without tools, fire, or clothing. He
could not trap, hunt, or kill. Instead he would have to forage
the leaves of plants as did the deer and lick dew from the
rocks and sand as did the mice. No shelter could be built, for
he had to wander, wander to the limits of starvation, thirst,
and fatigue. He was not permitted to speak or communicate
in any way with any being, not even with the Creator. To
all, he no longer existed, he was to walk as the dead. It was
his first trial, a trial of one long, waking, walking vision
quest, to show himself and the Creator that he was worthy
of the path of the shaman, to show all of creation that he

wished to walk this path more than he wished to live and that everything he owned, even himself, was sacrificed and dedicated to this path, this vision of visions.

In retrospect, Grandfather remembered only the first four days and the last seven. All else remained vague and dreamlike. Of the first four days he remembered vividly the fatigue, the thirst, the starkness of the landscape, and the intense heat of the sun, which seemingly burned holes into his soul. No one spoke to him; nothing yielded any sign or concern. Except for the perpetual pain and fear, he felt as if he had ceased to exist.

On the fourth day he remembered falling from a high ledge of rock, his body pounding into the sand below as if slammed onto a hot anvil. Then all reality was gone. Surreal images rushed to fill the void. Events and teachings, symbols and signs, ran by him at high speed, flooding his mind with a swirling mass of unconnected knowledge. He remembered long and short journeys of the imagination; he saw and spoke with spirit entities of animal, plant, rock, wind, and water. He heard the voices of many spirit things. He remembered knowing all things and then nothing.

He awoke many miles from where he remembered falling from the ledge. He noticed the autumn colors and realized that the season had changed, that he was several weeks beyond the time of his fall. His body was undamaged; he felt no fatigue, hunger, pain, or thirst. His once parched and broken skin was as soft and resilient as the day he had first seen the world. But he could not piece together the past weeks of forgotten travel or of the lessons he knew he must have learned along the way. And he realized that the hell of the barren desert could no longer affect him. He had been reborn, renewed, and had moved beyond the effects of comfort or pain. He now traveled easily, without the restrictions of flesh; his senses reached beyond human limits. He knew instinctively things of life and of creation that he had never consciously, willfully learned. And he understood that with the fusion of inner and outer dimension came a release from the exigencies of survival. There was only the balance, the harmony of his thought and spirit with that of the universal mind force. He had arrived at the sacred "oneness."

On the morning of the appointed day, he returned to the camp. The elders were amazed, for Grandfather's life force seemed to glow from deep within. Here he stood, fresh, relaxed, and powerful, unscarred from his ordeal. It was as if the Creator had taken his life only to send him back more alive than he had ever been, full of knowledge and power. From that day and for the next five winters he was schooled by the elders and he flourished. His lessons were learned quickly and effectively, and his tests and trials were undertaken with ease.

His knowledge of the old ways grew daily. But as months passed Grandfather came to see that the old ones could teach him no more, that all they could offer was a physical reinforcement of what he had learned intuitively on his first quest in the desert. The desert quest had certainly been mysterious, shocking sometimes, yet he never questioned the truth of the spirit world or of the Creator. He knew that all things were possible; he did not need to know why; all he needed was absolute faith.

Nearing the end of his training, the elders began to address him as Grandfather, though he was still in his early twenties. At first Coyote Thunder called him Brother, but it wasn't long before he, as the others, called him Grandfather. He was given all the honors of an elder and he traveled frequently into the wilderness to quest and pray, or to heal a distant patient. The group quickly learned to depend on Grandfather's wisdom and power for guidance.

It was when he returned from a long trip one day that he discovered his people gone. Not a mark of foot, fire, or lodge could be found. It had been swept clean by the fiery winds of the desert, and even his keen eyes failed to find a sign. At the center of what was once camp, however, was his scout headband and the staff of the shaman. Hanging from the lance in a circle were sixty feathers. He knew that the time had come, as his long-ago vision had declared, for him to wander—alone, far away from his people.

As Stalking Wolf pulled the lance from the ground, a coyote sounded from afar. He lifted his eyes, and there on a ridge in the misty distance stood Coyote Thunder. His great-grandfather waved a solemn good-bye, and Grandfather knew that this would probably be the last time he would see him. Coyote was very old, over one hundred winters, and health was failing. Suddenly there was the call of another coyote. The mists of the distant ridge cleared and where Coyote had stood there was a young boy, dressed in the clothes of the white man, collecting ancient stones, talking stones that spoke of ancient times. The boy stood and waved to Grandfather, as had Coyote; then he was gone.

Grandfather struggled to find the message of what he had seen. First there had been Coyote and then a boy— a white boy at that—playing with stones. It didn't make sense. But the land remained mute and unyielding, and a great loneliness filled him.

For over twenty years his small tribe had been his family. Now, because of his vision, he was forced into exile. This vision seemed to have no end, except perhaps in the wandering itself. Was there more? He knew that he would spend the rest of his life looking for the answer to this question. But for now he just sat at the old camp, searching his thoughts for a place to start his journey, his quest. He lost himself for a while in the work of setting up camp, for here he decided to stay until the path revealed itself. That night he dreamed of a white mountain lion calling him back to the place of the original quest.

Before the morning sun broke the horizon, Grandfather had broken camp and was heading back to the place of the original vision. He hadn't been back to that place since the vision, and now he yearned to drink of its purity and isolation once again. There he hoped he would find the answers, or at least a direction. He traveled quickly, as a scout, avoiding all the potential dangers, real and imagined. His mind was fixed on that sacred place where it all began for him, for his father, and for so many of his people. The trek lasted several days, across desert, over mountain, and through forest. The terrain was tough, but his training easily carried him. Like the eagles soaring the skies, his trip was an effortless flight. It was sunset as he approached the final ridge that looked over the sacred area. As he neared the top, the memories of his first trip flooded forth. His spirit soared, his body trembled with anticipation—until his longing eyes broke the horizon of the ridge and his stomach sickened at what lay below.

There below him was sprawled a miners' town. Huge holes gaped in the earth and the soil was torn by the deep swathes of roadway. All about lay garbage, broken machinery, and muddy water, where once the stream had flowed fast and clear. Buildings were tossed about the landscape in a careless, haphazard manner, and the smell of rotten sweat and liquor filled the air. On the winds drifted the drunken laughter, arguing, and turmoil of the inhabitants. People stumbled from building to building, throwing bottles to the ground, laughing, shoving, and shouting. This sacred place had been destroyed, butchered. Trees had been cut, rocks moved, and the solitude destroyed. To Grandfather's horror, nailed on the front of a building was the gorgeous hide of a white mountain lion. A coyote sounded near Grandfather, and the people began firing guns blindly at the ridge where Grandfather sat. In a flurry of bullets, Grandfather slipped from the ridge and to the safety of the wilderness, his head spinning with disbelief, anger, and pain.

He wandered aimlessly for many suns, trying to understand these white people who had no regard or reverence for the natural things. Moreover, he did not know why the mountain lion spirit had called him back. Why? What reason could there possibly be in all that destruction and sacrilege? What reason could there be for him to be its witness? The more he thought about that sacred area, the more he knew that he had to go back and find the lesson in the destruction. Whatever the intent, he had to follow his dreams and visions, seeking their wisdom no matter how painful. It was an incomplete answer, but it was the only direction he had right then, and he knew that no more would be given until he followed the one at hand. What troubled him perhaps even more was that he should have known something was wrong miles before he got to the sacred area. Had the sacred scout skills failed him or did the spirits blind him to the warning? He would return again to this diseased town, only this time as a scout, to get a closer look.

He used the cover of the night to slip back to the town. He knew that where there were villages, there would be men scattered throughout the surrounding area. The nuances of the night foretold of people coming and going all around him, but he could sense their apprehension, their inability to blend with the landscape, especially at night. He was secure in his skill and at home in the wilderness of darkness. His trip went easily; not a bird or beast sang of his arrival. To all concerned, he was invisible.

A few hours before sunrise, he arrived at the ridge overlooking the town. Below, everything was silent. Like a phantom, he slipped down to the street, passing the horses and dogs without a sound. Nothing stirred to his presence. The main street was thick with the smell of manure and the stench of unclean men. Garbage, rotted food, and broken bottles were strewn about, making travel slow and difficult. On the raised wooden sidewalks, men slept the blind sleep of drunkenness. Some lay clutching bottles, others were clutching guns as if in subconscious battle with the night and all its imagined terrors. Grandfather easily passed through town, searching every alley, peering into windows, and gazing into the open holes of the mines. He searched for answers to the questions of his heart, until the sky turned from black to the dark blue of approaching dawn, when he returned to the ridge, to a small fissured cave to sleep, escaping the eyes of man.

He awoke late in the afternoon, judging by the action of the birds. The sky was dark and overcast, the distant hills misty with rain. He slipped back to the edge of town, hiding momentarily in a dilapidated tool shack. From his vantage point he could see the comings and goings of the towns-people. Grandfather noticed how restricted their movements were, how square, boxlike houses and heavy clothing cut them off from the elements. It seemed they saw nothing of the natural world—eagles soared overhead unnoticed. They lived in a vacuum, separated from everything but themselves and the squalor they'd created.

These people seemed so strange. They didn't blend with the wilderness but feared it, holding it at a safe distance, like a man handling a deadly snake. They had no regard for the land, animals, plants, or even water. Litter was freely tossed. Live trees and brush were carelessly cut from around the dwellings. Unnamable waste was everywhere. These men were worse than their domesticated animals, living in their own filth, having no other purpose, it seemed, than to fatten and die. Laughter was usually drunken and at the expense of others, otherwise there was none. The faces of this village looked so pained and distorted with sadness that Grandfather wondered what directed these lives into this septic existence. So many questions filled his head. Why did they wear heavy clothes against the reality of nature? Why did they cloister themselves in sterile houses, rush about so aimlessly, or take such great time and care with simple processes of survival? Their lust for comfort, security, and safety seemed almost barbaric. It was foreign to Grandfather's thinking that anyone could consciously insulate themselves so lavishly from the wilderness and life itself.

Grandfather's attention was drawn to a young boy, a Native American but of uncertain origin. His hair was crudely chopped, and he dressed in old ripped clothing of the white man that was far too big for him. His walk was labored and clumsy in the heavy boots, not at all the fluid and silent gait of his ancestors. He was stumbling around a wagon while unloading bundles onto a deck. One of the bundles burst and spilled onto the muddy street. A large white man who had been standing on the platform the whole time began screaming at the young man, finally kicking him in the chest, then throwing him facedown into the mud. Other people began laughing at the boy as the man beat him with a whip. As the boy collapsed in pain and humiliation, the group of men went inside the building. Grandfather stared on in horror, for they had treated that boy worse than they treated their animals.

Rain began falling hard, casting the village into the darkness of cloud and mist. The boy lay in the mud, as still as death. Grandfather could no longer contain the rage and anguish that flooded his heart. In a flash, he slipped from the shed, then under one of the buildings, finally to the deck beside the young man. He carried the young one back to the old toolshed and threw a blanket over him, nursing him back to consciousness. The young boy opened his eyes for a moment, trying to orient himself, then without a word fell back to sleep. Grandfather waited for night, lashed together a travois, and dragged the semiconscious boy to a distant cave, far away from town. He made a fire and a warm bed of debris. When he had made sure the boy was in a comfortable sleep, he slipped back out into the night to hunt food.

The next morning the boy awoke with a start, disoriented. His face and chest held old scars of past whippings and the fresh scars of yesterday's lashing. The boy was afraid that he would be hunted and killed, but Grandfather put his mind at ease. It took a while for the boy to relax enough and accept Grandfather's caring, but somewhere deep inside his forgotten heritage the boy instinctively trusted Grandfather's medicine and power. He had been taken from his parents when he was very young by the man who had beaten him the day before. He had been treated like a slave, a beast of burden, and a whipping post. He was forced to sleep with the animals and forage for rotten scraps of food. Escape would mean a certain death because the man would hunt him down and kill him as he had others before. The boy, having none of his ancestors' skills, also feared the prospect of survival in the wilderness. He had never been trained in the old ways, but deep inside he could feel the pull of the pure and natural world, an existence far from the insanity of what he was living.

Grandfather learned much from this young boy; all the horrors of the white suppression, all the restrictions of reservation life, the starvation, the disease, the drunkenness, and the child stealing. He learned that the old ones were not even allowed to practice their religion, nor could they hunt for food. Instead, they had to live imprisoned on lands that could not support them, where the winters were cold enough to kill elders and children, and the summers were full of thirst, scorching heat, and killing disease. White Indian agents grew fat and rich by hoarding the government food and clothing that was meant for the reservation. Disparate tribes were thrown together, warriors were tortured or killed, and quickly the old ways were being destroyed. The once proud tribes were disillusioned and broken; hopelessness and helplessness had become the rule.

The boy went on to describe the white man's religion and how no two whites would agree on what was right. They had forced their religion upon the people, and though this religion held many truths spoken, rarely did the whites live the truths they espoused. Their black robes might speak of peace and love, but their lives were struggles of greed, power, and war. This only confused the people more, and the elders who turned their backs on the teachings of the whites were cast aside, beaten, starved, and even killed. The young ones were sent away to distant schools to learn the white man's ways, only to find on their return that they were unable to live in either world. Treaties signed in good faith were met with lies and deceit and, in the end, the prison of reservation.

The whites were strong in numbers, as well as weapons, but proved enormously weak in their ability to live with the earth. And because they feared the earth, they called it wild and forbidden, something to be ruled and civilized. The young Native American begged Grandfather earnestly to train him in the old ways, so he could live away from the hell of the white world. Without hesitation Grandfather agreed.

At that moment a coyote howled from a distant ridge, thunder rolled across the sky, and Grandfather knew why he had been led back to this place. He had seen the insanity of people living against nature, and he had seen the cruelty that this isolation brings. He had seen the children of the earth lose their skills and beliefs to the suppression by the whites. He knew that someday the white man would have to pay for his sins.

Grandfather took care of the young boy for more than a moon. He nursed him back to health and taught him simple survival and stalking skills and introduced him to the ancient spiritual truths. During that time they moved camp farther back into the hills for safety as encounters with people from the village were becoming frequent. Once the boy was strong enough to travel and had mastered the basics of escaping detection, Grandfather decided to move north and to the mountains. Before leaving, however, Grandfather went to the village one last time, saying only that he had to free the lion. That night he entered the village once again, stalked through town, and climbed the building that held the white mountain lion captive. He cut the skin down, praying and making ritual offerings as he wrapped it carefully into a buckskin bag. He slipped from the village, leaving this once sacred place to the cancerous insanity of the whites. He felt the urge to stay and fight for the sanctity of the place, but he knew that fighting would not produce anything but pain and hatred. So with a reluctant heart, he looked now to the high purity of the mountains.

Grandfather spoke often of his years in the mountains, wandering up into the heart of Canada, then back again to the southern reaches. For a few years the young Indian stayed with Grandfather, learning the old ways until his skills were sufficient to keep him alive anywhere. He eventually took a young Indian wife and retired into the wild upper reaches of the Canadian Rockies. Grandfather visited them whenever he was near their home, until the young man was killed while bringing his baby to a mission for help. Some local farmers had mistaken him for a thief as they saw him running from the mission with a bundle in his arms. The bundle was his infant son and both father and child died in the same senseless flurry of bullets. Grandfather never understood how anyone could feel that any possession was worth a human life. Thief or no, the young Indian should not have had to die.

It was about the time of the young Indian's death that Grandfather left the sanctuary of the high, rugged Rocky Mountains and began living in the deserts. Like his life in the mountains, he pushed his skill to perfection, practiced the spiritual teachings, and vision-quested. Whenever possible he would seek out the elders of tribes in the area, learning whatever he could and sharing his knowledge. Some of these old ones became lifelong friends and guides, and he would visit them often in his travels. Many times he would sneak onto reservations and gather a group of children, teaching them the old ways of skill and spirit. Often, however, he was run off by the whites and sometimes the Indian people themselves. So brainwashed were they about the taboos of the ancient ways and what the repercussions of learning them could bring that they kept their children from them. But more places than not, he and his teachings were welcomed.

Again and again, another calling, another vision, would lead him to other lands. His spiritual quests led him to the West Coast, up to Alaska, down the center corridor of the Great Plains, to the Mississippi Valley, up the East Coast again, then back down through Mexico and into Central America. In his wanderings Grandfather crossed this country many times, and always he was learning, seeking the things of the spirit, and pushing himself beyond his limitations of yesterday. He would settle in and learn an area only until the next vision pushed him on. But even where he did settle, there was little rest, for he was always a scout, living secretly and undetected, fearful always that he would be caught by whites and sent to a reservation or worse. With few exceptions, he stayed away from the white people. And as he grew older, he sought only the company of the wilderness and the spirits, rarely visiting even the elders.

He wandered for the better part of his life. Everywhere he traveled he witnessed the senseless destruction of the earth and his people. Like an unchecked cancer, the devastation quickly grew out of control. No place seemed safe, untouched, not even the rugged, hidden areas, the places in which as a young man, he had always sought refuge. The more he witnessed, the more he despaired of fulfilling the calling of his vision, of becoming a great and inexhaustible teacher. Willing students, young or old, were increasingly difficult to find in this fast-changing society. And many of those who seemed willing were at best only curious and not willing to put in the work and sacrifice needed to learn the old ways properly. Modern society had produced people who thrived on instant gratification, on lightning-fast and easy learning. Their new values were foreign to the teachings of the earth. He was growing old and running out of time; his desperation, loneliness, and despair were intense. His vision had led him to a weariness beyond old age. There seemed to be no end in sight to the helter-skelter folly of modern life.

It was at this pinnacle of despair and old age, when his vision was fading, that Stalking Wolf decided to end his life. He felt as if the spirits had abandoned him, that he had not followed his vision properly, that all was lost. So he wandered back to his homeland to find his people and decided that if he found them vanished like so many others, he would end his existence. He wanted no longer to see the destruction of the earth; he would rather live out the remainder of his years with his people or not live at all.

His long path brought him back to the ancient sacred area where he had had his first vision—the place of the ancient scout, the white mountain lion, and the white coyote. As he crested the ridge, he expected to see the squalid village once again, but to his amazement it was gone. It had vanished from the face of the earth in the flames of fire, the drying winds, and the erosion of time. Hardly a scar was visible. Nature had reclaimed what was once hers. And his heart soared.

He set up camp near the same rocky outcropping where he had his vision. Here he felt safe, and here he wanted to stay until he died. As the sun set, a lone coyote moved to a distant ridge and released its long primal cry of loneliness, and thunder rolled across the clear sky. Grandfather stood trembling, knowing it was a calling from his great-grandfather. More coyotes and more thunder joined in until the night vibrated with their callings, then all fell silent. The ancient warrior appeared as he had many years before, vivid and strong, standing out from the blazing horizon like he was cast in stone. He motioned to Stalking Wolf. Then, as before, he motioned to the east, only this time with more power in his command. Coyote's body turned to shadow, then evaporated, leaving only the pointing hand. Grandfather gazed toward the east. A small boy collecting ancient talking stones turned and looked at Grandfather, then smiled and became a white coyote that finally lost itself in the final flicker of sunset. Grandfather headed east. By plan or design, I was collecting fossils that day by the river when I saw Grandfather. I smiled, feeling that I had known him forever, and in the distance I heard a coyote howl. Grandfather smiled with tears running down his cheeks, but I was too young then to know why.

That was all that Grandfather revealed about his life and vision for a while. We could clearly understand his driving force and how he had no choice but to live his vision or die. We were amazed at the sixty-three years he spent wandering and searching, sacrificing everything that most people would normally cherish. He had no real home except for wilderness, and no possessions other than the truths of his heart. It would be many months before Grandfather revealed the many things that happened to him during those sixty-three years of wandering, but for this night we had enough to understand, and we began to understand him.

2

A Different Drum

Rick and I were always at odds with society. There were
two different worlds as far as we were concerned. There was
the reality of Grandfather's world of nature and spirit and
there was the phony sterility of the world of society. Rarely
would they agree with each other and this sometimes put us
into horrible predicaments. We were torn between doing that
which was right in the natural world and that which went
against what we believed just to keep peace in the world
of society. This conflict never seemed to be resolved, even
in the smallest ways. What Grandfather taught us, what we
knew of the natural and spiritual laws, and what we knew
to be true in our hearts did not fit into society. What society
generally taught us did not work in the pure and natural
world. It only worked in the games people played.

It was not long before Rick and I began to lead a dual life.
We learned that we had to play the "game" just to be able
to function in school or around people. We had to remain
silent about the many things we learned in nature and of the
spirit, especially of the spirit world. There was no doubt in
my mind that we would be ridiculed if we even came close

to saying anything about what we knew in the spirit world. It was bad enough that many people looked at Rick and me as rather odd. They could not understand why we spent all of our spare time in the woods, especially with the old man. They began to treat us at times like we had some disease or were abnormal in some way. It was not long before Rick and I said nothing about the woods or what we learned there. In fact we began to avoid the subject altogether whenever we were around our peers.

Once when I was still very young and just getting acquainted with the ways of the spirit, I was held up to horrible ridicule. I had found an arrowhead in the back section of our playground at school, in the thick out-of-bounds area of the schoolyard. Many of the kids saw me emerge from the off-limits area with the arrowhead and wondered why I had been back there. Not only had I violated a school rule to pick up the arrowhead, but when questioned by the kids and the teacher I told them that a spirit voice had directed me to it, innocent to the fact that I was saying something bizarre. To me, it was quite natural to be guided by my inner vision and I did not understand why the kids laughed so hard and the teacher sent me directly to the principal.

The principal did not believe a word that I told him. In fact, he seemed to be very concerned that I had heard some voice calling me. He told me that it was just my imagination and that I probably had brought the arrowhead from home to give me an excuse for going out of the playground. He sentenced me to three days of after-school detention. What was worse was that the kids would not stop mocking me, saying that I had imaginary friends. This ridicule followed me home to my folks, who accused me of lying to the teachers. It was a turning point in my life because from that day on I would tell no one of spirits. To me, up until this point in my life, I thought that everyone used their "inner vision" or heard the spirits speak.

That weekend in the camp area with Grandfather, I told him what happened in the school playground and what the teachers had said. I told him that I was concerned that I might be some kind of freak to imagine voices, after all none of my friends did. I also told him that they thought that I was a little strange, even crazy, and I was ridiculed often for it. Grandfather smiled at me and said, "You found the arrowhead didn't you? Was it then the voice of your imagination that directed you to it or the voice of a spirit? If there was no arrowhead to be found, then it would be your imagination. But it was found, thus the voice is truth. It is always the end results which tell us if something is spiritually real or just imagined."

He then went on to tell us that he too had gone through what we were going through though not in such a bad way. Generally Native American people as a whole, even children, accept the spirit voices and the spirit world without question. It is part of their reality. Yet children even in a highly spiritual society can also be cruel, as Grandfather found out. He too had felt that he was strange at first and would not even mention the things that occurred on a spiritual level to anyone, not even the elders. He thought that he might be imagining the spiritual things that he saw. Some of the things that happened to him were even grander than the spiritual things that happened to the elders and he thought it would show disrespect.

Grandfather said that his first spiritual encounters were in early childhood. At first, it began with a distant drumming in the wilderness. When he would go to investigate who was playing the drum, there would be no one there. Several times he found evidence of an ancient encampment, but no drummer. He also began to hear a drumbeat different from the one that was being played at the ceremonies he attended. It was in perfect cadence with the beat of the real drum, but where there should have been only one real drum being played, he sometimes heard one, two, or more different drums. He could pick the location of each invisible drum and sometimes even feel the vibration. Sometimes he could even feel the swish of the drumstick.

Grandfather did not want to tell anyone of what he was hearing and experiencing. He did not know whether the elders could hear or feel the other drums or if they heard drums in the wilderness where no one was playing. He would watch people's reaction at the ceremonies, or watch expressions when he heard drumming in the wilderness, but there was no indication that anyone took notice. Once in a while an elder would smile off toward the direction of the drumming, but then go quickly back to what he or she was doing. Sometimes he would even allude to drumming to people, without being committal, but all he would receive were strange looks. Some people would tell him that he was hearing things.

It was not long before Grandfather began to believe that he was really imagining the drumming rather than it being a spiritual experience. So too did he begin to believe that there might be something wrong with him and his thinking. Possibly, he thought at times, it could be an evil drumming and it could be luring him into evil. He grew very upset and confused over all that he heard. For a while he tried to shut off the drumming anytime he heard it, but he could not get it out of his head once it started. The drumming encounters went on for the better part of a year, then finally disappeared. There was a period of several moons where he received no sound of distant drums, not even during a ceremony. At this point, he finally felt that his imagination had created all that he heard.

Many months after Grandfather had heard the last of the drumbeats, he was exploring a small ridge far away from the main encampment. It was late in the day and the sun was starting to set as he headed back to camp. The sun cast the landscape into deep shadows and enlivened the colors of the desert, adding a sense of mystery to the day. Grandfather paused for a while to enjoy the sunset and to pray, as was his custom at that time of the day. Even at a very young age, the children of his clan were taught to set aside sunrise and sunset for personal prayer and introspection. This was always a special time for Grandfather, especially enhanced by sunsets that fired the sky. He always poured his heart into his prayers, always devoted his full attention at these times to the Creator.

As he prayed, he began to hear a distant chanting from the ridge right across from where he was seated. At first he thought that it might be one of the elders in his daily devotions, but when he opened his eyes to look across the small valley to the other ridge, no one could be seen. The chanting, however, continued without stopping. He thought at this time that the singer of the chant could be just beyond the ridge, out of his line of sight, so he set out to find that person. Though in waning light, he was still able to climb down from the ridge easily and make his way across the valley quickly, then just as quickly climb up the other ridge.

The closer he got to the origin of the sound the louder it became, but suddenly as he climbed to the top of the ridge the chanting stopped.

To his horror and amazement, there was no one there. In desperation, fearing that his mind was playing tricks on him again, he searched the dusty ground for footprints. There were none to be found, anywhere. There was no evidence of any human tracks in the area other than animals, not even old human tracks. In the now darkening sky, he feared that he may have encountered an evil spirit that lured him to the place, but the area did not feel of bad medicine. Still, he hurried quickly back to the main encampment, just in case it was of evil origins. As he ran, he was determined to tell the first elder he saw of the chanting he had heard, but then as he drew closer to camp he decided not to, for fear of being ridiculed as a scared child.

He began to contemplate the chanting as he neared camp. It was in a language that he could not understand, a language and cadence he had never heard before. He was certain that there had been no ceremony of his people that came close to what he had heard and that became his main reason for not telling the elders. Still, he was concerned that the chant may have been of evil origins, and though he could repeat every word, he drove the chanting out of his consciousness. There was no way that he wanted to be called a foolish child, or be told that his imagination, coupled with the fear of the dark, was playing tricks on him. The thoughts of the chanting troubled him all evening to a point where he was afraid to walk into any dark shadows around camp.

That night, in fitful sleep, his mind became filled with all manner of bizarre dreams. He dreamed of an old man sitting on that same ridge, looking out to a similar sunset as he had seen that evening. The old one did not look evil, nor did he do anything evil, he just appeared to sit and pray. Several times he heard the chanting again, sometimes coming from the old man on the ridge. Twice he was awakened from sleep by the chanting, so that he could not determine whether he was hearing the chanting in his dreams or in reality. All the time, the chanting remained the same. His night was truly tormented, and filled with fear.

With the light of dawn, Grandfather felt his fear now being replaced by curiosity. Certainly the light of day could drive away the unknown fears born of darkness, but his curiosity was strong yet still cautious. He was determined to go back to the ridge and find out if the chanting was still there. He wanted desperately to know if the chanting was truly from the world of spirit or if it was his imagination, and whether it was good or evil. So after his camp chores were done, he set out alone to go back to the ridge and see if the chanting came again. He did not want to go there with anyone for fear that they would think him stupid for what he was attempting to do.

He spent most of the afternoon searching the ridge from which the chanting had occurred. In full light there was no evidence of any other human being on top of the ridge. Only his tracks from the evening before and other animal tracks could be found. He began to wonder if the chanting had occurred from a different location, producing an echo, that he assumed to be the place of origin. Fully suspecting that this was the reason behind the chanting, he began to search all around the ridge, but again he could turn up nothing that indicated any human had been there. In fact, he did not even find any old tracks belonging to man.

Finally, as the day moved to dusk, he climbed back to the top of the ridge where he had first heard the voice. Sunset again was a spectacular fire and the landscape was rich with deep color and shadow. As soon as he began to pray, he heard the chanting again and he opened his eyes with a start. On the distant ridge, he clearly saw the image of an old man, the same old man he had seen in his dreams of the night before. Just as quickly as the chanting had started, it stopped again, and the image of the old man quickly disappeared. Grandfather blinked several times and even changed his position to make sure that his eyes were not playing tricks on him.

Sure now that the old man was moving away from the ridge and back to camp, Grandfather quickly jumped down from the ridge, crossed the valley, and climbed the ridge, determined to catch up with the old man. Upon reaching the top, the old man was nowhere to be found on the open landscape. Grandfather desperately searched again for tracks but to his horror there were only his tracks from the afternoon to be found. He wondered if it might be that he had seen a large animal and mistaken it for a man, but upon searching he found no large animal tracks. He was so afraid at this point, even more so than on the night before. He suspected that because he heard a chant that he did not understand that this old man must be evil. He panicked and ran back to camp.

Just before reaching camp he slowed his pace and composed himself. He did not want to show his peers that he might be frightened coming in out of the dark. As he entered camp, the image of a man appeared before him, sitting on the ground cross-legged. He jumped back from the image with a yelp of fear and suddenly the man spread wings and took to silent flight. It had been an owl that sat before Grandfather, and such was the poor depth perception that night brings, he thought that it had been a distant sitting man and not a close owl. He laughed to himself at how his mind had played a stupid trick on him and suspected that was what had happened back at the ridge. After all, he had never thought to check for the tracks of large birds. Satisfied with that explanation he decided right then to go back to the ridge the next day and look for tracks of large birds.

By noon of the next day, after a full and virtually dreamless night's sleep, he was back on the ridge checking for tracks. He tried finding any evidence of bird tracks all around the area where he had seen the image, but there were none. He even searched out farther and farther, but again there was nothing of significant size. He then began to believe in his heart that it had all been a trick played on him by his imagination and that it was probably a play of shadow on rock. As far as the chanting was concerned, he did not know. He could not blame it on the wind for there had been no wind. All he could do was speculate that it must be from the world of spirit. Good or evil, he did not know, but no harm as of yet had come to him so he thought it must be a good spirit.

Later that evening the chanting returned to the ridge, but this time it was not long before it vanished. Several other times he visited the ridge and each time at exactly the same time of evening he heard the chanting. Then one day it was gone and the ridge was quiet and imageless. Grandfather visited the ridge time after time but the image or chanting did not return, nor did his mind play tricks on him. At this point he had to just resolve himself to the fact that this mystery would never be solved as to whether it was from flesh or spirit. With each subsequent visit to the ridge, his fear diminished until there was no longer fear of the ridge.

Almost a full moon after the last time Grandfather visited the ridge he returned, this time with a friend. His friend, called Stone, was a few years older than Grandfather, nearly ten, an age when most boys were thinking of manly pursuits and usually didn't play with the younger boys. However, Stone and Grandfather played along the ridges most of the day, forgetting that age was any factor at all. They played stalking games where each would try to stalk the same animal. The one who got the closest or actually touched the animal before it took flight would win the match. By the day's end Grandfather had won nearly all of the matches, and it made Stone very angry that a younger boy could beat him at a stalking game.

As it grew near to dusk, Stone began to realize that he would not catch up to Grandfather's score and began to get even more angry, almost abusive toward Grandfather. But Grandfather was having too much fun to take notice of Stone's change in attitude. Suddenly, as Grandfather and Stone were in the process of stalking a deer, Grandfather heard the chanting again. This time it was stronger and clearer than he had ever heard before. Such was the clarity of the chant that Grandfather abruptly turned his head in the direction of the ridge and this caused the deer to bound off. At that point, Stone also turned his head and looked in the same direction as Grandfather was looking, then looked back toward Grandfather in a questioning sort of way, but clearly angry.

Stone was angry at Grandfather because at the point where Grandfather had turned his head and spooked the deer they were both even in the stalk. He could have won that stalking game because Grandfather was facing a wall of brush and Stone's path was clear to the deer. Without thinking, Grandfather asked Stone if he had heard the chanting too, as he motioned to the distant ridge. Grandfather had assumed that because Stone had also turned his head that he had heard the chant. Stone burst into a rage, calling Grandfather a liar. He told Grandfather that he had just done that because he knew that he was losing the last stalking game. He demanded to be called the winner and Grandfather complied. But Grandfather asked again if Stone hadn't really heard the chanting.

All the way to camp, Stone, realizing that he was far behind Grandfather in the stalking game, began to mock and taunt Grandfather about hearing imaginary voices. Stone figured that by doing this he would diminish his own defeat while making a mockery of Grandfather. He called Grandfather a frightened little child with a stupid imagination, telling him that he had no right to be walking with a real man. Only children imagine voices and pretend friends, especially when they realize that they may be losing a game. He also accused Grandfather again of cheating and lying, taunting and mocking him all the way to camp. As they neared camp other boys joined into the mockery, coached on by Stone. Grandfather at this point was almost in tears, but anger had the upper edge.

Finally back at the outskirts of camp, Stone pushed Grandfather to the ground and began to drive his face into the dirt. Grandfather struggled but could not free himself while the other boys began to yell and scream at Grandfather for being a cheat and a liar, a child who had no right to be around true men such as they. Tears began to fill Grandfather's eyes as he struggled and failed to free himself. Seeing his tears, the boys began to feign crying and called Grandfather a baby, now with even more vigor. Their cry of harassment finally filled the camp and several elders ran to break up the fight. Grandfather at this point was weeping openly and was very humiliated. Stone broke free of the elders' grasp and pushed Grandfather to the ground again, causing Grandfather's mouth to fill with blood.

Again the elders broke up the fight and demanded to know who was the cause of it in the first place. Stone immediately blurted out the whole story about Grandfather hearing the imaginary voices and spooking the deer, failing of course to say that Grandfather was far ahead in the game. One of the elders turned to Grandfather and asked him if what had been spoken was true, and Grandfather reluctantly agreed, but tried to explain. The elder cut him short with a wave of his hand and told Grandfather that it was not in the spirit of a true man to lie and cheat. With that they all began to walk away, leaving Grandfather to his humiliation and tears. At one point Stone turned back around and made a rude gesture toward Grandfather and smirked in triumph.

Upset and angry that the elders would not listen to his version of what happened, Grandfather did not know what to do other than to sing the chant. As soon as he began to sing the first line of the chant the group stopped abruptly and the oldest of the elders looked back at Grandfather in absolute amazement. This old one was considered to have powerful medicine and as soon as he turned back so did the entire group. Picking up on the chant, the old one sang along with Grandfather until the song ended. Still held in amazement and with tears in his eyes he asked Grandfather where he had heard the song. Without hesitation, Grandfather told him of the ridge. The old one simply smiled and said, half to the group and half to Grandfather, "This is a very old song I learned as a boy. It is not of our people and has been lost all of these years. The boy speaks the truth. He is not a cheat and a liar." He then just turned and walked away, the rest of the group slowly following.

Nothing more was said to Grandfather about the chanting, not even by the elders. He did notice a change in the way that the elders treated him from this point on. There was always a warm smile from all of them whenever he passed, a warmer smile than normal. So too did his peers treat him a little differently. Certainly they still played games, but they somehow kept him apart, as if he were different in some way. Grandfather began to feel that they felt that he was peculiar. So too did he begin to think that many people in the clan were talking about him when he was not around, and this made him feel even more self-conscious. Yet, as the weeks passed nothing more was said about the chanting that Grandfather had heard.

After a while, especially since he was not again confronted about the chanting, Grandfather figured that the elder had only said what he said because he instantly knew Grandfather was probably insane. Yet he could not explain how the elder had picked up the chant right away. He also began to sense that other people were watching him, especially the elders. But when he would catch them staring out the corner of their eye, they would quickly look away when he looked at them. Those he did catch watching him would always give him a warm smile and a wave. Sometimes he would even catch sight of someone following him when he went out on his walks. When seen they would act as if they too were just out for a walk or involved in doing something else.

This was an especially confusing time for Grandfather and he began to spend more and more time wandering alone. He rarely played with the other children after a while, not so much because they didn't want to play with him, but he didn't want to play with them. He was more than content to just wander by himself, exploring, and spending time within himself. So too did he find that the elders were talking to him much more than they had in the past. They showed more than a keen interest in what he was doing and where he was going. His great-grandfather was especially instrumental in encouraging him to get out by himself, many times doing the chores that Grandfather would have done.

At first, even on his longest and most remote walks, Grandfather no longer heard any drumming or chanting, not even along the ridge where he had originally heard the chant, though he had been back to the same place many times before. Once when he sat on the ridge and looked over to the Chanting Ridge, as he called it, he spotted the old elder medicine man there. The old one sat near the exact place he had seen the image of the old man chanting and he wondered to himself if it were not the old elder who had truly been responsible for the chant. After all, he was the one who knew it when Grandfather had sung that chant. Yet even during the time that the older elder prayed there, there was no chanting. The only strange thing that happened was that the elder waved back to Grandfather when he left, never looking around to confirm that he was there.

It was shortly after the older elder was spotted on Chanting Ridge that Grandfather began to hear the drumming again and soon chanting that went along with the cadence. It was miles from Chanting Ridge and on a barren strip of land where Grandfather could see for miles around. Again there was no one to be seen from the direction that the chanting and drumming were coming. So too was it in the middle of the day and there were no shadows or obstructive land formations to affect his view. He listened for a long time and to his astonishment it was a different drum and chant than he ever heard before. Several times the drum changed cadence and even the chant was modified or changed, though he could not clearly make out the words.

As if driven more by deep spiritual desire than by physical means, he began to wander in the direction of the drumming. The farther he went, the louder the drumming and chanting, until it felt like he was surrounded by it. He sensed that he had somehow walked into the center of an invisible circle, such was the way the sound surrounded him. So too did he begin to sense a presence of some kind, followed by some faint and quickly disappearing images of people moving or sitting. Then as suddenly as it all began, everything vanished. Grandfather was left to the vast emptiness of the open plain and with his deep sense of confusion and wonder. He trembled from the intensity of the experience, though vowed that he would not tell anyone what he had witnessed.

For the many weeks that followed this incident, Grandfather began to experience drumming and chanting almost on a daily basis. So too did he begin to encounter the images of more and more people but they did not seem to want to communicate with him. He still did not know whether he was imagining all of this or whether he was having real spiritual encounters. Still, he would not breathe a word to anyone. He was afraid of the elders' reaction to all of this; in fact he was afraid of any reaction at all, whether positive or negative. He knew from what he had heard that spiritual encounters did not come easy to people. Many would have to go out on a vision quest to even come in contact with the spirit world; many more would have to be deeply involved in a ceremony. To Grandfather it all came so easily and he feared that it would offend those who had to work hard for spiritual encounters.

It was during one of Grandfather's trips out alone when he was startled by a man standing alongside the path. The image of the man was so transparent that he had to look hard to keep him in his line of sight. He stood for a long time in fearful amazement, until the spirit approached and stood before him. The spirit looked at him for a long moment, then spoke, saying, "Tell the wife of Owl Man Dancing that he is alive, but he is badly hurt and needs help immediately or he will die." With that the spirit went on to explain to Grandfather exactly where Owl Man Dancing could be found and that he should hurry and get help. With that the spirit fell silent, then vanished.

Grandfather, without question, began running back to camp. He knew that Owl Man's wife had been worried when he had not returned from a lone hunt. He was a week overdue and she feared that he was dead. As he approached camp, he slowed his pace to a painful walk, being torn between telling what the spirit had told him and not wanting to be considered a fool again. As he walked into camp, he decided not to say a word to anyone. That was until he saw Owl Man's wife crying in front of her lodge, being comforted by several elders. Without hesitation he ran up to Owl Man's wife and blurted out what the spirit had told him. Grandfather no longer cared at this point what anyone would think or say and he was more than ready for their questions.

To Grandfather's amazement, everyone began running, arousing the camp for help, and heading, without hesitation, in the direction that Grandfather was told that Owl Man would be. Grandfather was virtually left alone and people went about their rushed business without paying any real attention to him. He wandered off, wondering if those that he had told thought the person he spoke to was a real person and not a spirit. He began to be filled with all manner of self-doubt and thought what a fool he was going to be when they did not find Owl Man Dancing. He decided then to disappear from camp for a while, especially since the searchers would be back before nightfall.

The remaining hours of the afternoon were filled with anguish for Grandfather as he agonized over what he had done. He imagined that he would be considered insane, and would certainly be left alone from that point of his life on. Certainly, the people would not banish him from his family group, but he would be treated from then on very differently. As he walked in the dwindling light he was again startled to see the same spirit standing before him as had given him the message. The spirit smiled at Grandfather for a long time, then finally told him that Owl Man Dancing had been rescued. He said that Owl Man's leg was not broken and would easily heal over the next several months. However, he told Grandfather that Owl Man had been trapped by fallen rocks and that is why his rescue was so important.

He then told Grandfather to go back to camp.

. Grandfather reached camp by full dark, yet the camp seemed unusually active with singing, laughter, and unusual activity. It was as if the entire camp was in celebration, though it was not the time yet for any celebration that he knew of. As he neared the outer edges of camp he saw a huge fire in its center with many people gathered around it talking and laughing. There at the far end of the fire lay Owl Man, with his head resting on his wife's thigh. He had a huge peaceful grin on his face that showed his contentment. Others sat around him, touching him compassionately every so often as they talked. Clearly it was a celebration for the safe return of Owl Man, though Grandfather could see his bandaged leg. To Grandfather it was a grand relief to know that the spirit had been right. Not wanting to face any questions, Grandfather slipped quietly into his great-grandfather's lodge and fell asleep for the night.

The next morning Grandfather slipped out of camp early, before most people were awake. He thought that it would be better to let the excitement die down a bit before having to face the questions of the elders and his peers. After walking all morning he finally headed back to camp, passing along the way several of the younger women who were gathering wild edible plants along the trail. They smiled at him and said good morning, but nothing more was said. When he returned to camp, all was as if nothing had happened. No one pressed him for any answers. In fact, no one mentioned the return of Owl Man at all, and definitely no one thanked him or acknowledged his tremendous role in the safe return of Owl Man. Not even Owl Man's wife said anything other than to give him a warm smile. It was as if he had no part in it at all.

This kind of treatment confused Grandfather and he began to imagine that he may have dreamed the whole thing. This went on for days, but finally Grandfather gave up and put the whole thing out of his mind. After a few weeks passed, he had nearly forgotten the whole incident altogether. Grandfather returned to his normal long walks alone, along with the increasing frequency of spiritual encounters, but there was no communication as had been with the spirit that had warned of Owl Man's peril. Grandfather felt a little used by the spirit world for if what had happened had not in fact been a dream, then they certainly were not helping him with his problem up until this point. He had always heard that the spirits were there to guide people, but now he felt abandoned.

Possibly, Grandfather thought, he might have done something wrong that he did not know about and that is what angered the spirit world into silence. The more he thought about it, the more anguish he felt. Finally he just gave up and no longer paid attention to any spiritual encounter. Anytime anything spiritual happened he would go out of his way to avoid it or push it out of his mind. He just no longer cared, the frustration had become too much. He even began to stop going on walks and kept himself busy with camp chores or learning new skills, or practicing the old ones. He used the work as a mandala for clearing his mind, removing his consciousness from his mind to his hands whenever possible. He chose to avoid the whole thing rather than to deal with it anymore.

He noticed a concern arising from the people, especially elders, about his behavior. They began to tell him to stop working around camp so much and to get out and wander like he used to. Some actually came close to begging him to go, telling him that he did not look happy. Grandfather had to admit to himself that he was not happy at all staying so busy. He would rather be out wandering and exploring on his own, but he just could not face any more spiritual encounters. Then finally an elder approached him one morning and just told Grandfather that people seeking spiritual things were always faced with many frustrations. But they had to learn to rise above the frustrations, and seek spiritual wisdom at all costs. Without further comment the elder just walked away.

This statement shocked Grandfather because it had taken him by surprise and had come without prompting. Most of all, it was exactly the answer that Grandfather had been looking for. Without delay he headed back out to the Chanting Ridge area and began to pray earnestly for the first time in many days. He poured himself into his prayers like never before, asking the Creator to forgive him for giving up so easily. He also begged forgiveness of the spirit world, and begged them to help him. He stated that he wanted to know this world more than anything else he had ever wanted in his life, and that he would from that moment on dedicate his life to that quest.

As soon as those words were uttered he heard the chanting once again, clearer than he had ever envisioned before. As he opened his eyes from the place of prayer he was amazed to see the original old man who had stood on Chanting Ridge standing before him. Next to him sat a drummer, keeping a slow methodical beat while smiling at Grandfather. The old man stopped chanting and lovingly put his hand on Grandfather's small shoulder. His touch was soothing and Grandfather felt his spirit surge with excitement. The old one said, "Tell the elders that you are now ready, and give the old one who sang my chant this," as he motioned to the ground by Grandfather's feet. Then suddenly all images were gone, leaving Grandfather alone, staring at the empty ground.

Grandfather was truly amazed and shaken by the encounter. Yet looking at the ground, all he saw was earth and had no idea as to what the old man had pointed to. Grandfather knelt on the ground and looked closely at where the Chanting Man had pointed. There, almost completely buried, was a buffalo effigy that was once part of a necklace. He carefully dug out the effigy and tried to preserve the strap, but it had rotted to dust. The effigy looked very old to Grandfather and he knew that he had to see the elders without further delay. He rushed back to camp without fear of any ridicule for he knew in his heart that Chanting Man, as Grandfather now called him, spoke the truth.

He walked into camp with a purpose in his stride, so much so that some of the people stopped what they were doing and watched him pass by. He walked directly to the elders' meeting lodge and paused at the door. He heard his great-grandfather's voice call to him to come in. Somehow it did not shock Grandfather that they knew he was coming. Grandfather stepped inside the lodge and was confronted by many of the elders sitting in a vast circle around a small fire. Shafts of sunlight poured through the smoke hole and made the room look mysterious, filled with a shadowy mix of smoke. The elders all looked at Grandfather, seemingly excited over what he was about to say.

Grandfather approached the elder who had sung the chant along with Grandfather many months earlier. He stood for a long moment, trembling, then finally said, "Chanting Man told me to tell you that I am now ready, and he gave me this to give to you," as he reached out and handed the elder the buffalo effigy. He sensed the deep hush in the room as the elder closely examined the effigy. The entire group, including Great-grandfather Coyote Thunder, seemed to wait in breathless anticipation for what the old man would say. No one was more filled with anxiety than was Grandfather at this point. He actually felt his knees shaking, such was the intensity of his anticipation.

Finally the elder spoke, saying, "Once again the boy speaks the truth. It was as we all had suspected. This effigy was that of my great-grandfather, Chanting Man, and he also knew the words of his sacred spirit chant. It seems that we were all correct. The spirits have chosen this young one and now we must begin teaching him immediately. He has passed the test of dedication, and now he seems ready." With those words the elder turned to Grandfather and said, "We left you alone for a long time after we realized that you possessed the gift. We wanted you to have room to grow spiritually on your own, and everyone knew to give you that aloneness. Now it is time for more aloneness and a long hard path, which you have already resolved yourself to taking." With those words Grandfather left the lodge knowing that he was somehow different from most others, listening always to the drumming that no one else can hear.

What I learned from Grandfather was that I had to also follow the distant drums, regardless of what society thought about the validity of spiritual things. I knew that I would not be accorded the luxury that Grandfather had, living among highly spiritual people, so I had to take greater care in covering my tracks spiritually. He taught me that just because others did not listen to or understand the workings of the grander spiritual world, it did not mean that I should turn my back on my path and my vision. After all, it was obvious that this modern world where I lived was far different from his. In this society things would never be accepted that could not be proven by the flesh. I also realized that if we as a people are to ever emerge from the flesh to the rapture of true spiritual enlightenment, then we must nurture the calling of the spirits.

3

The Stone Vision

Rick and I were camping near the top of a high dome in the Pine Barrens that we called Fossil Hill. Our main ambition on this particular camp out was not to practice our survival or tracking skills, but to explore the areas around the hill. We were especially interested in collecting more fossils for our collection. This hill was rich in the type of gravel beds where fossils could be found. Mostly the fossils were formed during the time that the Pine Barrens lay under the ocean, thus they were fossils of small shells, coral, and other fragments of marine life. We would lie on these gravel beds for hours, meticulously searching out the best stones. We would become so engrossed in what we were doing at times that we would be completely oblivious to anything going on around us. This day was no exception.

Though there was rarely a competition between Rick and me as we learned the skills of survival, tracking, and awareness, there was a competition when it came to collecting skulls and fossils. Our individual collections were so enormous that they had moved beyond the confines of our rooms and began to collect in the basement and in the attic. At times our competition became so fierce that we would fight over skulls or fossils that we both saw at the same time. In our minds, our wealth was measured in the size of our collections and the rarity of its pieces. Many times before we began a collecting expedition such as this one, we would have to lay down ground rules that dictated when and where we could collect. This would prevent us from infringing the other's territory.

Still, setting aside all competition, Rick and I would work together and help each other, holding mock conferences as to how we could approach a possible fossil-rich area. The excitement of one of us finding a rare fossil in good shape became the other's excitement. We probably found more joy in finding a tiny fossil than did an archaeologist finding the complete skeleton of a wooly mane mammoth. Lying on our bellies and exploring the micro landscape of gravel would produce hundreds of adventures and bursts of excitement in a single day. By sunset, Rick and I would be exhausted from all the excitement, though neither of us would have moved more than ten feet in eight hours. Our eyes would burn and our heads would pound with pain from looking so close. Our bodies were stiff, cut, and scraped from lying in the stones. But the joy and satisfaction transcended all pain.

On this particular camp out, we had collected all day Friday and most of the day Saturday. Now on Sunday, we were back to work again in the lower beds. Our collecting bags bulged with all that we had found. As we lay on our bellies and searched the ground we discussed the work of identification and labeling that lay ahead. This would certainly keep us busy on the many school nights that we were not allowed out after dark. The care and maintenance of our collections were always a source of escape when we were confined to the house. Our conversation drifted to many topics that morning, but as usual it terminated with the discussion of finding the "mother lode."

In our imagination, the "mother lode" lay somewhere beneath us. It was an illusory bed of fossils that were unexposed, whole, and rare. This bed would contain hundreds of fossils where we could not pick them up fast enough. We talked about how we would explore such a bed, how we would collect the stones, and ultimately the travois we would have to build just to get the fossils back to our homes.

In the few short years and the many hours we had been collecting fossils we had yet to find such a place, but we knew they had to exist. In many of our archaeological books there was reference made to these special places, yet try as we might, we could not find one. We couldn't even come close. At best we would find two or three fossils lying in the same small area, and that was considered a rare find. The more we talked about this "mother lode" the more our passion grew for finding it.

As we were lying on the ground, Grandfather came by to watch what we were doing. He called fossils "talking stones," and told us that they were the voice of the past. He too showed a definite fascination with the fossils but would never collect them. Instead, he would find a good fossil and admire it for hours, studying it at every possible angle. At times he would press the stone to his cheek, taste it, or hold it to his ear and listen. I imagined that he was actually listening to some faint voice that we could not hear. To me it actually appeared as if he were talking to the fossil and listening to what it had to say, such were his actions. It always captivated me to watch him sit for hours with a single stone, while we greedily gathered so many. He always appeared so satisfied with just one.

What was so perplexing to me was the way that Grandfather would find a fossil. He didn't have to lie on his belly and search for hours as we did. Instead he would walk right over to a stone and pick it up. It was as if he saw the stone from many feet away and knew right where to go. What was most exasperating was that he would always find the most beautiful and whole fossil, one that could easily become our most prized piece. This day was no exception; no sooner had he arrived at the fossil beds when he walked over and picked up a stone. Rick and I immediately quit what we were doing and ran over to see what he found. We knew from past experience that it would have to be beautiful. As we gazed into his hands and at the stone I gasped. It was a perfect fossil of a trilobite.

This made me a little angry and frustrated, for in the few years that I had been collecting fossils I only found a partial trilobite and even that was in poor shape. Now in Grandfather's hands lay a perfect specimen. It baffled me as to how he could walk right over to an area I had searched the previous day and pick up such a stone. It was as if the stone were calling to him. We each begged Grandfather for the fossil when he was done with it, and Grandfather could sense the tension growing between Rick and me. He looked at the stone, then at us, and then bent over and picked up another stone just in front of us. He then handed me the stone he had just picked up and the trilobite stone to Rick. My eyes began to fill with tears of disappointment until I looked at the stone that Grandfather had handed to me. It was another trilobite as good if not better than the one he handed to Rick. I was amazed.

Rick looked at me with a smug expression on his face, as if to say he had gotten the prize, that is until he saw the joyful expression on my face. He walked over to me and we compared stones, trading them back and forth so that each of us could savor the beauty of each other's stone. We could not believe how easily Grandfather had found the stones, and lying right next to each other. We both looked at each other and simultaneously said "mother lode" and dropped to our knees, eagerly searching the ground where Grandfather had found the stones. We searched the area vigorously for the better part of an hour but could not find a single fossil. Grandfather watched from afar, giggling to himself about our frustrated searching antics.

Finally, after satisfying ourselves that there were no more fossils in that area we wandered over to where Grandfather was sitting. To our utter amazement he was studying another perfect trilobite fossil. We could not believe that Grandfather had so easily found another; it was impossible. I thought to myself that if I could learn what Grandfather's secret was for finding these fossils, I would become fossil rich. Sheepishly, I asked Grandfather what he did to always find such beautiful fossils. He smiled at me knowingly and said, "I talk to the stones and I hear them call my name. The stones then tell me where the best are to be found."

"But how do I learn how to talk to stones?" I asked.

Grandfather smiled again and said, "You must first give your life to the stones, then and only then will you begin to understand their language." I asked Grandfather what he meant when he said to give my life to the stones, and that is when he told me his story of the talking stones.

When Grandfather was still quite young, and long before he became a man in the eyes of his culture, he learned the wisdom of the talking stones. Grandfather was always more than impassioned with learning the practical skills of surviv- al, tracking, and awareness, but he could see no connection between those physical skills and the wisdom of the spirit. Though he had often heard the elders say that survival was the doorway to the earth, and awareness was the doorway to the spirit, he still could not fully understand the connection between flesh and spirit. There was something that was missing in the connection, something that he had to learn before he could fuse the consciousness of flesh and spirit. He knew that there was a connection, an answer, but he did not know how or where to look.

For more than a year, Grandfather had been commu- nicating with the world of spirit, but he still lacked that deep connection to the entities of creation. He could not understand why it had been so easy for him to communicate with the spirit world and why it was so difficult for him to commune with the world of nature. In his mind, it should be the opposite way. Certainly he could feel the connec- tion, but that connection came hard. Communication was always random and incomplete at best. He so often heard the elders speak of "the-spirit-that-moves-through-all-things," a collective consciousness that we are at once part of and "one" with, yet he could only touch it at times and never fully communicate with its power. The elders, however, could fully communicate with the trees, the plants, the animals, and all entities of the earth.

Grandfather began to grow very frustrated with his search for the connection, for the voice of creation. He would sit for hours, sometimes for days, in front of a rock, a tree, or a body of water, but nothing would speak to him. He felt that the world of physical creation was ignoring him. The herbalists of his clan told him that they knew what a plant was to be used for by simply asking the plant, but no plant seemed to speak to Grandfather, at least not when he wanted them to. Here too the communications were random and rare, only coming to him when he absolutely needed to know. It seemed to take almost a life or death situation before anything would talk to his heart. His search for answers became a lesson in desperation and frustration, to a point where he could think of nothing else.

In utter desperation, Grandfather finally approached his great-grandfather and told him of his plight. He had hesitated for so long in going to the elders, for he feared that they would think him inept. After all, he had so freely communicated with the spirit world and now would possibly look foolish because he could not talk to the entities of creation. He told Great-grandfather Coyote Thunder of all the times he had tried and failed to communicate with the various trees, rocks, plants, and animals, and of how miserably he had failed. Coyote Thunder listened attentively and patiently to Grandfather's plight, smiling at him lovingly. Then after a long moment he told Grandfather that he would have to give his life over to the rocks. He said, "The rocks are the oldest and wisest people, for they are the bones of Earth Mother, from which all soils and all life comes. It is the rocks and stones you must seek for your answers."

Grandfather had no idea of what Coyote Thunder meant when he told him to give his life to the rocks. Contemplating the rocks, he decided to take what he called a "stone vision quest." Possibly this is what Coyote Thunder meant when he told him to give his life to the stones. After all, he assumed that the vision quest was like dying, and if he could surround himself with rocks and stones, then it would be like giving his life over to the rocks. He searched for days, looking for just the right location for this quest. He decided that it was not enough to just be surrounded by rocks, but he had to be "in" the rocks. To be "in" the rocks he knew that he would have to find a cave and do his vision quest there. That way, he would in essence give his life to the rocks, or so he thought.

After several days of searching he found just the right cave. It was very small, and high up on a mesa. He was barely able to fit his body through the opening. Grandfather could not stand or even sit in the cave, for the only way he could remain inside was to lie on his back. Even then, he could not turn over unless he went outside the cave and reentered in the position he wanted to lie in. He thought that this would bring him the closest he could ever come to being "in" a rock. His flesh would fuse with that of the rock, such was the confinement of the cave. In essence, it was like lying in a rock coffin. So too was the crawl into the cave very long and difficult. It would take Grandfather more than an hour to force his way to the back of the cave. There was no light after the first bend, and he had to feel his way into the depth. He prayed the first time that he went in that there were no rattlesnakes along his route.

After several days of fasting and praying about his vision quest, he left before first light. It was difficult to climb up the face of the mesa in the dark, and he had to feel his way to the mouth of the cave. Grandfather had to listen attentively before placing his hands on any ledge, for fear of a rattlesnake resting there. Any slip would surely mean his death, but his determination to quest transcended any fear. It took him several hours of climbing before he reached the cave, and then he was so exhausted from the climb and from the previous days of fasting that he trembled with fatigue. All he could do was to lie at the entrance in utter exhaustion and pray, such was his pain. It was first light before he could even bring himself to enter the cave.

The crawl into the cave took far longer than he ever imagined. At the first turn, he encountered a coiled rattlesnake. He had to wait utterly motionless until it finally slipped by him and out to the entrance. As Grandfather slowly worm crawled his way to the back of the cave, all of the difficulty he thus far encountered began to weigh heavy on his mind. It did not feel right to be there. In fact, it hadn't felt right since the beginning steps of his quest. But he knew of no other way to give his life over to the rocks. It seemed that even the very cave itself wanted to vomit him out. Even after reaching the back of the cave, he could not get comfortable. It took several times going in and out just to find a tolerable position, but even then he found it very difficult to breathe.

It seemed that everything from that point on tried to drive him from the cave. At first, difficulty in breathing had to be overcome, and only after shifting his position for another time was he able to get enough air flow past his body to make breathing tolerable. In the depths of the cave it was very cold and he found it almost impossible to stay warm without shivering. He could not see at all, such was the darkness, and it was impossible to gauge the time of day, or even whether it was day or night. Finally, the going and coming of various animals in the cave entrance kept Grandfather on edge. Several times he thought that he heard the slithering of a snake and twice he heard a definite rattling at his feet. Still, he was determined to stay in the tomb of the cave.

He thought that it was not the fact that he shouldn't be questing in the cave, or doing something wrong, but more that the rocks wanted to test him to see if he was worthy of their wisdom. It was an utter hell for every little annoyance distracted him from his quest. At times the tight conditions created an intense claustrophobia that took him to the edge of panic. He fought hard at times just to stay put. He knew that this panic would only distract him more than anything else he had yet encountered and that panic became his biggest mental fight. This struggle against distraction seemed endless, where even sleep became impossible. He had no idea how long he had been in the cave, but it felt like days had passed by. Logically, however, he knew that he could not have been in the cave for over half a day.

He found that by holding his head hard against the side of the cave he could see past his body and toward the mouth of the cave. He could make out a faint light coming through the entrance of the cave, and he knew that it must be just high sun. He then realized that he had only been in the cave for several hours, not days, and the disappointment that swept over him was almost unbearable. It was not in his consciousness to ever give up and soon his despair turned to an almost violent determination. As far as he was concerned he resolved to remain in the cave even if he did not get any spiritual communication from the rocks. His determination tended to border on uncontrollable anger at himself for giving in so easily. If torture is what he had to go through to get any wisdom, then torture he would endure.

It seemed that when Grandfather became determined to stay in the cave no matter what he had to endure, the distractions lost their power over him. He could think more clearly and for the first time he felt a certain peace. Time then seemed to slip by unnoticed as his mind wandered over all manner of questions about the rocks. In fact, the next time that he looked toward the cave's entrance, there was no light at all. Not even the stirring of a rattlesnake shook him anymore. After all, if a rattlesnake did bite him, then it had to be for a reason and he no longer cared of the consequences or fear of such a bite. Instead, the slithering sound and the intermittent rattles seemed more like music than a threat. It was only when the snake struck and the unseen prey squeaked, that it shook his concentration.

He watched the faint light come and go from the cave's entrance. Though he did not actually know how many days had passed, he assumed it had been at least two. Though he did not sleep at all, it was hard at this point for him to discern between waking and sleeping. The sensory deprivation of the cave became so overwhelming that he not only lost time and place at times, but lost his perspective between vision, dream, and reality. At times he remembered being very lucid and alert, but most times he existed in some other state of dulled consciousness. Even after he fell into his first deep sleep, there was still no sharp line between reality and the surreal. Eventually he gave into trying to discern between awake and asleep and no longer allowed himself that luxury of knowing.

At the point of what he thought was the third day he heard a rapping sound coming from outside the cave. At first he did not know what the sound was, such was the intensity of the echo inside the cave. But upon listening carefully he decided it was the sound of two rocks being hit together. This sound kept up for a long time. At first it was very rhythmical and lulled him into a stupor, but eventually the sound became erratic and annoying. After a while it became hard for him to concentrate on anything else and his anger began to return. The more the hammering kept up, the angrier Grandfather got. He began to imagine that it was some of the very young children from camp, playing around the base of the mesa. He tried to scream out, but the sound continued.

Exasperated and angry, Grandfather began to back his way out to the entrance of the cave. He thought that if he was to ever be able to get in touch with the rock people he would first have to put an end to the hammering. Finally at the entrance of the cave, eyes burning from the glare of daylight, he looked across the bottom of the cliff. There was no one to be seen and the noise had disappeared altogether. He began to wonder if he imagined the sound, but as soon as he began to crawl back into the cave, the sound resumed.

Gazing out across the landscape again, he realized that the origin of the sound was not from the ground but from the top of the mesa. He shouted out again, but the sound continued. Infuriated and more frustrated than ever, he crawled to the top of the mesa, determined to yell at the children for disturbing his quest.

As he finally reached the top of the mesa, he was surprised not to find children, but one of the elders of the clan, working on some stone tools. With his anger dissipating now, he began to approach the elder in a humble way. He was going to tell the elder of what he was trying to do and to ask him kindly to work in another location, though he did not want to seem disrespectful. As he approached the old man working stone, the elder looked up at him and smiled warmly. Without waiting for Grandfather to speak, the elder said, "I knew that I would find you here." His words took Grandfather by surprise, but he said nothing. The elder spoke again, saying, "You must give your life to the rocks, not die within the rocks," and with that the old one handed Grandfather a cutting tool that had been chipped from stone. Without another word the old one walked away and left Grandfather to his silent contemplation.

Grandfather was dumbstruck. He was amazed that the old one was actually looking for him. Confusion began to saturate his every thought. What did the elder mean by giving himself to the rocks rather than dying within the rocks? Could all of this frustration in the cave have been from the fact that he was going about this in the wrong way? Was it that he had misunderstood what Coyote Thunder had originally told him? And what did the elder mean anyway by giving his life to the rocks? The clue, he realized, must be in the stone cutting tool that the old one had given to him. It was then that Grandfather realized what they had meant. By giving his life to the rocks, he had to rely solely on the rocks for his survival. It was obvious to him now and he felt so stupid for not understanding in the first place.

Without delay or returning to the encampment, he wandered out onto the desert, carrying only the stone that the elder had given to him. After he was out of sight of the cave he removed his loincloth, his bone knife, and the small bag he always carried with him. This would be the first time in his life that he would have to face a full survival situation without any tools. Usually on his excursions into the wilderness he would carry with him his bag and his knife, but now he faced the wilderness naked. So too did he decide that he would have to also leave the stone tool that the old man had given to him. That way he would have no ready advantage and have to make everything from scratch, even his most basic tools.

Certainly he was well versed in the survival skills, but this would be the first time he ventured out with nothing. His survival excursions had been limited to a few days at best, and even then they were under controlled conditions. In a way, Grandfather was a little apprehensive, because he doubted his own skill. He felt so frail and insignificant as he entered the vastness of the desert. So too was this wilderness one of the most formidable that he had ever known. The longer he walked, the more vulnerable and alone he felt. He began to doubt his own skill till eventually his apprehension turned to fear. Still, he was determined to learn the wisdom of the stones. After all, he had since wasted two or three days in the cave, and that made him more determined not to waste any more time.

Once Grandfather found a suitable place to survive, he set about building a shelter and finding a source of water. Near to where he built his shelter he found a damp area near the bottom of a mesa. There he was able to dig down a few inches and the water began to seep in. Now all he had to concern himself with was to build a fire and find food. He knew that with shelter and water he could stay alive for many days, but if he was to last out more than that he would have to take care of the other necessities. That is when he knew that he would now have to give his life over to the rock people. His chore then was to find and form a rock that would help him to carve the materials he would need to make a hand drill. As he searched out the perfect rock, he began to realize that without that rock he would never be able to make a fire and it would be difficult if not impossible to build the hunting weapons and traps he would need to gather food.

He searched all afternoon, but all the rocks were many miles back at the mesa area. All that surrounded him were endless sands and chunks of soft rocks that easily crumbled when he attempted to hammer them to shape. As dusk began to overtake the land, he grew desperate and tried to make his hand-drill fireboard and drill with the crumbling rocks, but to no avail. He even attempted, as the last light disappeared from the sky, to bite the pieces into shape. At best, he was able to bite a crude cut in the drill, but one that he knew would not work. He realized at this point that he would have to spend the night without fire and with no food. It was too dark now to wander off into the landscape and find any edible wild plants. He knew that he should have brought the stone cutting tool with him that the elder had given him. He should have known that he would not be able to find suitable tools this far out in the sand lands.

The next morning after a miserable night with fitful sleep and chilling temperatures, Grandfather set out to find the chipped tool that the elder had given to him. The desert had grown very cold that night and the shelter that he had built was designed to have a fire inside. He knew that he would have to find the stone or spend another miserably cold night in his shelter. It took him several hours to reach the place where he remembered leaving the stone, but upon his arrival he could not find it at all. He searched along his path, but still he could not find any trace of where he had left it on the previous day. The stone had virtually disappeared altogether. His search began to take on a desperation as the day moved into dusk. It quickly became obvious to Grandfather that he would have to spend the night where he was, and abandon his search for the stone until the next day.

Night was moving in fast and Grandfather knew that he would have to hurry to build a shelter that would ward off the chilling night air of the desert. The area he was in was devoid of any suitable vegetation that could be used for a shelter. Most of what he found was sparse. If only he could make a fire, he would be at least able to survive the night with a relative degree of comfort. Giving up the possibility of making a shelter he decided instead to fashion a hand drill and try again to make a fire. He broke bits of dead brush and tried desperately to bite the drill into shape, but to no avail. He tried to cut the notch into the fireboard, but every fragment of stone he found soon crumbled into dust. He tried to make the fire with the crude apparatus time and time again but failed even to get smoke. If he were to survive the night he would have to find some fragment of stone that would work.

Shivering in full darkness, he lay on his belly and began to run his hands deep into the sands, searching for even the smallest stone. Temperatures began to plunge even colder than on the previous night and he began to shiver uncontrollably. Normally he would fair much better but with the previous days of fasting his energy was dangerously low. It became clear that he might not be able to survive the night and there was no doubt that he would have to find a stone or perish. He could not venture a walk back to the mesa, for he would be dead before morning. He had to conserve what little energy he had left. The only thing that stood between him and death was to find a stone, any stone, large or small, that could be used to cut wood without crumbling.

With trembling hands he began to intensify his feeling search of the sands. He was now reaching a point of panic, for the sands would produce nothing but the crumbling stones that he had used before. Several times he would find larger pieces of sandstone, but even they were of no use when he tried to file the notch into the fireboard. Tears began to pour from his eyes as he cried out to the Creator for help, but it seemed that even the spirit world had turned its back on him. He felt so alone and vulnerable, and the frailty of his life seemed to be magnified by his fast approach to freezing to death. In the darkness, he could feel his mind swirl with all manner of thought, nearing nightmare or hallucination. Shapes began to move across the distant landscape and he had to shake his head to make them disappear. He could barely hold on to consciousness.

It was at this point of panic and hallucination that he began to remember why he was here. It was to give his life to the stones so that he could eventually understand their communication. He cried out into the dark, asking the unseen stones to help him live. It was then that Grandfather noticed a faint sparkle in the distant sands. It was as if a small fragment of star had fallen to earth and illuminated the sands. He feebly crawled to the small sparkle of light. He tried repeatedly to shake his head and drive away the hallucination, but the sparkle continued. As he drew closer, he saw that the sparkle was coming from a large piece of sandstone. Picking it up to examine it with his fingers, he found that embedded in the sandstone was a small hard pebble, the kind that could be used to cut a notch. Though this little stone was far smaller than he would have liked, he had to attempt to use it for the cutting.

He broke away the sandstone and dislodged the small pebble. To his delight, it had a sharp edge along one side. Though the edge was only the length of his pinky nail, he knew that with a little time and effort he would be able to cut the notch. He knew that time was what he had very little of so he quickly located the fireboard and began abrading away the notch. His shivering made the work very difficult and at times he could not hold on to the stone hard enough to make it cut. He talked to the stone unconsciously, asking it for help, and thanking it profusely with each good cutting stroke. Finally, almost near the edge of utter exhaustion, the notch was finished. With his last remaining strength, Grandfather began to spin the hand drill and within moments began to get smoke.

He could feel the excitement and relief begin to emerge from deep within him as he began to blow the tinder into flame. Tears filled his eyes as the tinder exploded and firelight flickered. Debris and sticks were added to the tinder and he could feel the warmth of the fire cutting deep into the cold of the night. As he felt his body grow warmer and the shivering stop, he held the stone to the firelight and thanked it profusely. That tiny little chip of stone had saved his life and for the first time he felt a definite communication between himself and the stone that bordered on love. Grandfather finally understood what the elders meant by giving his life to the stones. This night, so close to the edge of death, he had truly given his life over to the stone, and it had saved his life.

Grandfather spent the next several days on the desert. He began to find the proper stones easily, for he was beginning to understand their language. He used the stones to help him build fires, make traps, prepare wild edible plants, and do so many other things. Grandfather finally understood that without the stones he would quickly perish, and deep inside a bond was formed, a bond of love and understanding for the stone people. That night, in a real way, the stone had spoken to him and sent him a sparkle of light in the cold darkness. Grandfather could feel that this communication was just the beginning of what would intensify and last a lifetime. One could not hope to speak to stones and understand their voice unless that bond was formed. That bond came from life at the edge of death.

As Grandfather told us the story of the stone, he took a tiny stone from his neck bag and handed it to me. I knew that this was the stone that had first saved his life. Though I had seen that stone so many times before, this was the first time I could truly understand what that little pebble meant to Grandfather. Up until then I thought it was just some strange and ugly keepsake. I also began to understand how Grandfather knew where to find the best fossils. All he had to do was to ask the stones and they would call his name. I knew that someday soon I would also have to give my life to the stones before I could ever understand their language or hear their voices. For me, the story of the stone would forever change my life. Stones for me became a living entity, so critical for survival, so important to understanding the deeper mysteries of life and spirit.

4

The Tree Speaks

Late one afternoon I was searching for a sapling that could be used for an arrow shaft. I was deep in the brush by the edge of the swamp near camp, and the searching process was difficult. I could have easily busted through the brush and broken things out of my way, but that was not Grandfather's way. We had to travel through the landscape like a shadow, disturbing as little as possible. We had been taught to be very careful in our travels, so unlike most people who crushed and destroyed things in their path without a second thought. We were taught that our impact on the land should be kept to a minimum, moving with the earth instead of against it. So my search became a combination of gymnasticlike movements and all manner of contortions just to move around things.

I had been meticulously searching for the better part of the afternoon when I finally came upon the perfect small sapling that I needed for the shaft. As I had been taught, I thanked the sapling for its life and teaching, then prayed to the Creator in appreciation for the gift of this life. I knew that each entity had a right to live and that each entity had

61

a spirit. I had learned long ago that there were no greater or lesser spirits. All were equal. The spirit of the ant was as important as a bear and the spirit of a blade of grass was as important as that of an owl. There was no spiritual arrogance in my heart, for I knew that all things were connected through the-spirit-that-moves-through-all-things. This fabric that makes up the collective consciousness of the life force makes all equal. Thus killing the sapling was like killing one of my own family.

After I had cut the sapling and begun to weave my way carefully out of the brush, I noticed that Grandfather was watching me from the edge of camp. I had no idea how long he had been there, but I assumed it was quite a while. I began to grow a little self-conscious, because he appeared to be a little disturbed by my actions. I began to wander back in my mind through the whole collecting process. I wondered if I had overlooked something or done something wrong. I knew that I had been very careful with my movements, and even more careful with the cutting of the sapling. Somehow I had done something wrong. I just instinctively knew it and my instinct was compounded now by the look on Grandfather's face.

I approached him sheepishly, like a naughty child who had been caught breaking some unknown rule. My guilt became almost overwhelming as I drew closer and his eyes pierced my very soul. I self-consciously asked him if I had done something wrong, or if I had upset him in any way. The look of stern accusation vanished from Grandfather's face and he began to smile. I was confused, for I was sure that he was dissatisfied with something that I had done. He smiled at me for a long moment, then finally said, "So you do somehow understand that you are guilty of breaking nature's laws. I can see it in your actions." I asked him what I had done wrong, for surely I had followed all of the spiritual and natural laws in the collecting of the sapling. He smiled again, and said, "It was not enough."

This statement really shocked me because I was certain that I had done everything he had shown me to do when collecting. My actions did not harm the earth and my heart had fully been in my prayers. I could not understand what Grandfather had meant when he said that it was not enough. Without waiting for me to ask the question, Grandfather said, "As I told you, we are caretakers of the earth. It is not enough to just remove the sapling and feel the thanksgiving, but there must be more, much more. Long ago, I told you the story of two men that were to go out and collect saplings for a bow. You only understood part of the story and have not fully become the caretaker. The meaning of your life here has not been fulfilled, for you have done only part of the work that needed to be done."

My mind raced back to the story that Grandfather had told me about the two men collecting bow staves. It was during a time when I had asked Grandfather if survival was detrimental to the earth. I had envisioned survivalists much like a swarm of locusts that devoured and hurt the earth. That is the way that most people looked at survival and I had to question Grandfather to see if it were true. It made me feel very guilty that I might be hurting the earth through survival living. Grandfather told me that there were two types of survival; that of the white man and that of the Native American. He said that the white man's survival hurt the earth, but the Native American survival helped the earth. He then told me the story of the two men collecting bow staves, to illustrate how different these types of survival were.

He said that when a white man needed a bow stave, he would just go out onto the land and take the finest and straightest sapling he could find. He cared little about what impact it would have on the land, nor did he care what he would leave for the future. As far as the white man was concerned, nature was put there for his use and his abuse. Land, water, animals, or plants did not matter. He fulfilled only his own needs with no thought to future generations or nature in general. Survival to the white man was a struggle between himself and nature. He felt that he was above the laws of creation and had dominion over the land. This survival destroyed the earth then and continues into the future. The white man's legacy has been adopted now by the global society, a society of people that kills its grandchildren to feed its children.

Grandfather said that when the Native American went out to collect a bow stave it was far different from the consciousness of the white man. First, the Native American had to have an extreme need for the bow stave. Then the collecting trip would be proceeded by periods of fasting and praying. After all it was not as simple as just cutting down a tree, for he would be taking the life of his brother. He would then go out onto the land and begin his search. He was not looking for the solitary saplings that grew straight and tall. Instead, he would search the groves of saplings that were in competition with each other. He knew that in their struggle for soil and sunlight many would die and others would be badly bruised and injured as the years passed. If left alone the forest would not be strong and healthy.

When such a grove was found he would search it thoroughly, looking for the ideal sapling. It would not be the straightest and tallest. Instead, it would be one that was dying or would eventually be crowded out by the other saplings. He would then ask himself if the land would be left better by removing the sapling. If so, then he would ask what kind of legacy would he leave for his children and grandchildren. Would it be a strong and healthy forest? Only when those questions were answered in a positive way would he eventually cut the sapling. Even then there must be the prayers of thanksgiving. His was the attitude of the caretaker, helping nature to grow better, stronger, and faster. He could do in a short period of time what would take nature years to accomplish. That was his purpose: to help and nurture creation, not to destroy it.

I had understood Grandfather's story about being a caretaker very well and I always followed that consciousness in collecting, but I could not understand what Grandfather meant when he said that it was not enough. What was I doing wrong, or not doing? Again, without waiting for me to ask the question, Grandfather said, "It is not enough to just take that sapling. Your vision is in a tunnel. You must look beyond the sapling and see what else should be done in the area to make the forest healthy. By taking care of a small part and not the whole, you are not doing enough. Your work as a caretaker has not been completed. It is also not enough to be the caretaker only when you are collecting something for survival. You must be the caretaker all of the time, whether collecting or not."

"But isn't that like playing God?" I asked Grandfather.

He said, "In a way it is, but we are only following the instructions of the Creator. After all, that is why we are here on the earth, to care for nature, not destroy it. You must take things from nature to live, that is a given fact, but it is the way that we take those things and the end results, both immediate and in the future, that make us caretakers." I thought about what Grandfather was saying, and I knew it to be true, but I could not be sure if we were truly following the wisdom and direction of the Creator. That is when Grandfather told me the story of the old tree and how he learned the wisdom of the caretaker.

It was just after Grandfather learned the wisdom of giving his life to the rocks, when he learned the lesson of being a caretaker. He was now learning to fully communicate with not only the rock people, but many other entities of the earth. He would sit for hours with a plant, rock, or animal that he had been drawn to through inner vision. He would eventually begin to understand their silent language conveyed to him through the-spirit-that-moves-through-all-things. The language, he quickly learned, was not in the tongues of man, but through the language of the heart. These communications would come to him through waking visions, dreams, signs, symbols, and feelings. At first these things were difficult to understand, but with practice they became as easy as any spoken language.

On this particular occasion, Grandfather was seated beneath an old and weathered tree, a tree that the elders called "The Grandfather." He had always admired the tree and felt compelled to go to it often, though there had not yet been any communication. It was a joy for him just to visit it regularly. He expected no communication from something as powerful as this respected old monarch. It would always fill him with such a sense of peace and contentment just to sit by its aged trunk. To him it became a symbol of nature's awesome power. Its sheer age and size made Grandfather humble and in awe. Even without any communication he could feel a bond forming between himself and the tree, a friendship that reached beyond all definition of fellowship.

Even though this old tree did not communicate with Grandfather he would still spend hours talking to it. He would discuss his problems with the tree, tell it of his adventures, ask its advice, and tell it of his triumphs and failures. He always felt so much better after talking to the tree and many times he found that he would gain answers and insights into problems by just discussing them with the tree. After many visits, the communications with the tree began, though he was not aware of it as a conversation at first. He began to learn its many moods, and how those moods would change with weather and other conditions. He could sense when it was sad or happy. He could feel its fear in a wind or lightning storm, and he could feel its joy on bright sunny days and during thirst-quenching rains.

On many of his visits to the tree, Grandfather would spend the entire day, and at night sleep beside its massive trunk. On one particular occasion, Grandfather had a powerful dream about the old tree, one which would change his perception of nature, and man's role in it, forever. Certainly, he had dreams while sleeping beneath the tree before, but rarely about the tree itself and never one so profound and upsetting. It was not that he had been seeking a vision during this time. The whole thing just happened without any provocation or forethought on his part. It came to him, however, after a day filled with questions about the spirit of nature, where Grandfather had been wondering if he could learn to communicate with nature more fully if he gave his life over to nature.

Grandfather was well aware of the fact that the only reason man could survive at all was through nature. Man without the raw materials to make tools could not survive at all. It was for man, he thought, a parasitic relationship, where man took but never gave anything back. Yet he knew that by giving his life over to the rocks, he had also in fact given his life over to the whole of creation. It was just that the rocks had become a connection to everything else. He was wrapped in a tremendous guilt about taking everything from nature and giving nothing in return. There had to be some justification to man's existence other than to just use nature. These questions and thoughts raced through Grandfather's mind as he fell to sleep beside the tree.

He began to dream randomly at first and the images seemed unconnected. He dreamed of past survival experiences, the trees he cut, the plants he had eaten, the animals he had killed, and the many rocks that he had broken. The dreams quickly turned into nightmares. Plants and animals began to scream out with fear at Grandfather's approach. As Grandfather walked through the dreamscapes he could feel the very plants begin to bend away from him. So too did animals flee from him in a blind panic. He began to feel that he was a disease that infected and ultimately destroyed nature. It was becoming clear to him that man was probably a mistake of creation, an entity that was dangerous and out of control.

His nightmare became more vivid. Now it was not only him that was destroying the natural world for survival, but many other people too. The accumulated effect was absolutely devastating. It was not the native people that he saw, but those people of the white race. Their effect on the land was even more destructive than he could ever imagine. Their lust for monetary gains left the land barren and beyond repair. They did not seem to care for the land at all or appreciate the many gifts of life that they were taking. Most of all they did not follow the rules of creation in anything they took from the land. The land did not matter to them. What mattered was only the present, and they destroyed the future for their children and grandchildren. The land cried out in pain and suffering.

He began to clearly understand the difference between how he and his people survived as compared to how the white race survived. He did not feel as guilty now as he had, for there was a disease on the land far worse than he. At least he did not ravage the land as these other aliens were doing. The natural world seemed so helpless, especially before the destructive force of man. At least the animals could flee but the trees and plants could not run. They were vulnerable and defenseless against the unstoppable force of man, especially the effective killing techniques of the white man. That is when Grandfather's nightmare turned to that of the old tree.

He dreamed that he was looking at the old tree from a distant vantage point when he saw people approach. He could feel the tree's trembling terror and he knew that the advancing people were intending to destroy the old tree. Unlike the animals the tree could not run or even try to defend itself. It was held fast to the ground and had to withstand anything that was done to it. With axes these people began to cut at the trunk of the tree. The chopping produced huge gashes in the bark and blood began to flow from the tree. The old tree cried out in pain but the people cutting paid no attention to its cries or its pain. The chopping continued endlessly and Grandfather could do nothing to stop them for he even feared for his own life, such was their viciousness.

Since the tree was so big, the people seemed to give up on trying to chop it down. Instead, now they climbed to the upper branches and began cutting these away from the main trunk. There too blood poured from the tree with cries of anguish and pain. The tree now shook with suffering, but still no one paid attention. Finally, Grandfather could stand no more. The tree was his friend, his Grandfather, and to stand by and watch the butchering and suffering continue was more than he could bear. Caring little for his safety, he rushed to the tree and began frantically pulling people away from the tree. No sooner did he pull someone away than another took his place. It seemed an endless stream of people, all determined to kill the tree.

In frenzied desperation now he began screaming at people to stop, to look at what they were doing, and understand the suffering of this old monarch. He was ignored completely, as if their lust to kill the tree destroyed their awareness to all around them. The cutting and hacking continued for most of the day, unceasingly. Grandfather tried everything to stop the massacre but to no avail. All he could finally do was to collapse in exhaustion and watch the old tree tortured beyond anything he could ever imagine. He could feel the tree cry out to him for help, but he was helpless. He cried in anguish, for he knew that he was losing this trusted old friend to the greed of man. These people felt no reverence for the tree, no remorse for what they did. In fact, they appeared as if they felt nothing at all.

Finally the chopping ceased and the people began to gather up some of the branches they had cut down. Soon they left the area, carrying the wood, but leaving much more behind. In all they but took a small portion of what they had cut from the tree, leaving the rest to decay on the ground. If only they had just taken what they needed, Grandfather thought, the tree would still have a chance to live. Now with all of its branches gone and its trunk badly hacked, it would stand no chance of survival. As Grandfather crawled to the trunk and wrapped his arms around part of its base, he could feel the tree dying. It wreathed in the final torture of pain, then slipped away into death. Grandfather had truly lost one of his best friends. His wailing cries awoke him from his nightmare and echoed across the night landscape.

Grandfather reached out and touched the trunk of the old tree, sighing now that it was only a hideous dream. The tree looked as strong and healthy as ever, but the images of the dream still lingered heavy in Grandfather's mind. He could still feel himself shaking deep inside. Even though he knew that everything was just a dream, it had left a lasting impression on him. He knew that it could be very possible that the tree could be cut someday, just as he dreamed. The horrible realization came over Grandfather that there was no way to prevent this from happening. The tree was helplessly imprisoned in the soil and could not run. It was vulnerable and helpless to the ravaging of man's destruction. He could not stand guard by the tree forever, nor could he hide the tree in any way. It frustrated him that he could do nothing to prevent its cutting from happening.

He even began to despise himself, for he was not really any better than those people who had butchered the tree. Certainly, he went about things differently than they did, but still nature was being used by him and was vulnerable to his needs. He understood full well that he had to take from the earth to live, but that still would not justify the way he felt. Man had an unfair advantage over creation, all take and no give. It seemed to Grandfather that this was a very one-sided relationship. It hurt him deeply that in one instance he could look to nature as kin, learn from it both physically and spiritually, then turn around in the next moment and kill that which he called family. It just did not make sense to him, because he could not really justify his actions, at least not in the way that he wanted. He could see no benefit that man had on the earth. At least animals and plants contributed to the overall scheme of things.

As he sat by the tree, his mind became saturated in these thoughts. It just wasn't right that man should be such a scourge on the land. He began to wonder again if man truly wasn't in fact a mistake made by the Creator. He was a disease, man was a disease, which seemed to have no real purpose. He looked toward the tree again, remembering vividly his dream. The tree looked even more frail and vulnerable. He felt the bond between him and the tree growing stronger, but he could also feel the fear that the tree felt. The overwhelming sense of helplessness overtook him again. At this point he even felt the paradox of his kinship with the tree. At once they were friends, but on the other hand if need be he would destroy the tree for his survival.

As Grandfather sat contemplating the essence of man's existence, Coyote Thunder sat down next to Grandfather. Grandfather had been so caught up in his thoughts that he did not notice Coyote Thunder's approach, and it startled Grandfather when he sat down. Coyote Thunder did not speak, instead he searched Grandfather's questioning eyes. It did not take Coyote Thunder long before he knew exactly what was going on in Grandfather's heart. He told Grandfather that he too had come to this old tree many years ago and was confronted with the same questions that Grandfather now wrestled with. Coyote Thunder said that he had felt the old tree's vulnerability and told Grandfather of a dream that he had, so similar to the one Grandfather just experienced. He told Grandfather that the tree was like a doorway to the answers, and many who came to the doorway were given the same questions and the same answers.

Without another word, he motioned to Grandfather to follow him. They traveled for the better part of the morning, deep into a mountain gorge. A beautiful stream cut its way deep into the gorge and they followed along its banks quite a way up the mountain. It was obvious to Grandfather that Coyote Thunder had come to this place many times before, such was his apparent knowledge of the area. Grandfather could also sense a reverence in Coyote Thunder for this place. It was not just another gorge, but someplace special to the old man. As they walked on, Grandfather began to see the landscape change dramatically. On one side of the stream the forest was healthy, tall, and strong, but on the other side of the stream the forest was bent, twisted, and many of the trees were quite diseased. It did not look healthy at all.

The difference in the two forests was quite startling to Grandfather. He could not understand why one forest was so healthy and the other so sick. After all the two forests were only separated by a thin ribbon of water. There was no evidence that Grandfather could see that would cause this remarkable contrast. Coyote Thunder said nothing but continued to walk slowly along the stream's edge. The farther up they went, the more dramatically different the forests appeared. The sick forest looked now as if it was barely able to survive, while the other looked stronger and healthier the farther he went. The healthy forest showed evidence of more animal tracks and the plants and trees had much fruit. Still, Grandfather could detect nothing on the landscape that would make one forest healthy and the other so sick and tangled. There was no sign of anything out of the ordinary in either forest.

Finally Coyote Thunder motioned to Grandfather to sit down. Coyote Thunder said nothing to Grandfather at first, but just sat and looked around with an expression of satisfaction on his face. Finally, he began to tell Grandfather the story of the forest. He told Grandfather that this was the place he would come to collect his saplings for bows and arrows. He had used this area many times in his youth, but now only came here to honor the forest. Grandfather looked around in utter amazement. Coyote Thunder had indeed helped this forest grow stronger than the other forest across the stream. Everything seemed perfect here, everything healthy. Grandfather told Coyote Thunder that it was one of the most perfect forests he had ever seen. Coyote Thunder only smiled and said that this was but one of many forests he had helped.

Coyote then began to explain to Grandfather man's purpose on the earth. He said, "Man is the tool of the Creator and creation. Man can help nature do what would otherwise take many years. Man belongs to the earth and the earth belongs to man. It is not just taking from the earth and giving nothing in return. As you see, the earth, this forest, once gave to me and I in return helped it to grow stronger. Man has an important part in the survival of creation, for it is through man that nature can grow strong and healthy. Do not the winds and storms trim the trees, do not animals eat the plants and other animals? Do the plant people not feed on the sunshine, the soils, and the waters of the earth? We all need each other to survive. But there must be a balance and harmony with man and nature. The forest here shows such a balance, it is the perfection of man's purpose."

Grandfather was beginning now to understand what Coyote Thunder meant by man's purpose for he could see the splendid results in this strong and healthy forest. Without waiting for Grandfather to ask any questions, Coyote Thunder continued, saying, "The problem is that the white man does not understand this balance and harmony. White man takes but never gives back. He is not a caretaker, but a disease that destroys the earth. White man does not know his purpose on the earth and thus is lost and searching for himself. Land to these people does not matter, for what matters is only their immediate survival. They care little of future generations or what their greed will do to the land. They have become contrary to the laws of creation and to fulfilling their destiny."

Grandfather sat and pondered all that Coyote Thunder had said to him, but more questions still needed answers. Coyote Thunder then said, "We must first understand that all things that live on the earth must eat. We must take things from the land in order to survive. It is how we take these things that makes the difference, that makes us caretakers and not a disease. We take things first with great thanksgiving and appreciation in our hearts for we must take a life in order to survive. We then must take that life in a sacred manner, in a way that will benefit the land rather than destroy it. We must look to the future and leave a grand legacy for our children and grandchildren. So too must we leave creation better than we found it; thus we fulfill our destiny as the caretakers of the earth."

Coyote Thunder continued, saying, "But our role as caretaker does not begin and end with taking the right things in the right way. We must become protectors of the earth. We must be willing to defend it with our lives if need be. So too must we always live the life of the caretaker. Nature needs our help all the time, not just when we are taking something from it. We must wander the lands, cutting, pruning, planting, and helping nature along, all of the time. So too are people part of nature and we must help them to grow stronger by teaching them and showing them the sacred ways. This is the best way we can protect that precious gift of life for future generations. However, many will not listen for they know no other way. The fight can become very long and hard indeed."

Coyote Thunder waited for a while so that Grandfather could fully digest what he was saying. Finally, after a long pause, he continued, saying, "Unlike the white man, we only take things when there is an extreme need. We are a people of simplicity, not excess or convenience. It is the consciousness of excess and convenience that produces the greed that ultimately destroys the earth. White man looks for this excess and convenience because he thinks that it will make his life simple and easier. This is not truth for the more white man tries to simplify, the more complicated his world becomes. He looks to the false gods of the flesh for the things he thinks will satisfy, but in those gods he only finds pain. There can be no satisfaction in a world of excess and destruction. We can justify our existence through that simplicity and thus help nature grow stronger, for now and in the future."

Coyote Thunder then walked off back down the stream, leaving Grandfather some time to think. Grandfather began to wander the forest that Coyote Thunder had helped to create. He also spent time in the sick forest on the other shore. He began to understand the great satisfaction Coyote Thunder must feel every time he visited this forest. He imagined the tremendous legacy that Coyote Thunder would leave for future generations. And for the first time, Grandfather could feel man's place in the scheme of things, and how important man could be to nature and for future generations. Grandfather felt so proud of what Coyote Thunder had done for the land. He could feel that same purpose growing within his own heart, and vowed to become a caretaker like Coyote Thunder, a full-time caretaker. He no longer felt like he was a disease, but a servant.

Eventually, Grandfather began to wander back along the stream and ultimately back to the old Grandfather tree. To his surprise, Coyote Thunder was seated by the base of the tree, leaning up against the trunk. Apparently he was waiting for Grandfather to return. As Grandfather sat down, Coyote Thunder said, "For a long time now you have separated nature from spirit. First you learned to listen to and hear the voices of spirit but you failed to hear those same voices in nature. Only when you gave your life to the rocks did you begin to understand. Now you must understand that there can be no separation of nature and spirit. They are one in the same. Nature becomes a doorway to the spirit and spirit also becomes a doorway to nature. There is only the sacred 'oneness' that we are all part of."

Coyote Thunder continued, "One last thought that you must understand. When we take something from nature, its spirit does not die. Instead it becomes part of our flesh and part of our spirit. There is no real death, at least not when things are taken in the right way, the sacred way. The only time that senseless death occurs is when things are taken out of greed and thus destroys the land. You belong and are part of creation's laws, and you belong to the earth, just as you are part of this old tree and it of you. Nature can exist without us, but it would struggle far more. Remember, we are here for a grand purpose, beyond self. We are the caretakers." Coyote Thunder stood up, smiled at Grandfather, touched the old tree lovingly, then began to wander back to camp. Grandfather sat in contemplative silence until nightfall.

As Grandfather wandered back to the encampment in the dark, for the first time in his life he felt so much a part of nature. He felt like now he could justify fully his reason for living, without regret. He knew that it was no longer a lopsided relationship, but an alliance that would benefit both him and nature. As he walked he felt so much closer to the entities of nature. He felt a grand communication begin and a new awareness that he had never known before. To him it was as if creation was welcoming him home, home as a savior and not a disease. He began to understand the essence of the "oneness" that the elders so often spoke of.

After hearing the story of the old tree, I could finally understand what Grandfather had meant when he said that what I was doing with the land was not enough. It was not enough just to be a part-time caretaker. The consciousness of being a caretaker must be foremost in mind and in action. It is not enough to just care for the land when we are taking something from it, but to constantly work to help nature along. No, we do not want to create a landscape like a well-sculptured modern park or garden. Certainly we want to keep it wild. But what we want to achieve is a perfection in nature, free of disease, healthy and strong. We must fulfill the reason we are put here on earth, and we can never do enough to help.

Today, I can see the ultimate impact of Grandfather's teaching of the caretaker attitude manifest in my students' lives. When we first leased our camp area in the Pine Barrens, the land was horribly out of balance. Poor lumbering practices had left the trees and plants in such bad shape that very little could effectively live off the land. The rabbit population was far outnumbering the carrying capacity of the land, twelve deer had died of starvation that winter, and the stream was choked and stagnant, devoid of fish. Today, after hundreds of students have passed through the area taking classes, the land is back in perfect balance. Our plants are back in balance, no deer have starved in the past seven years, and the stream is open and potable. Fish have returned and every year we get a vast crop of acorns, pinecones, and innumerable berries. It has become a Garden of Eden. What would have taken nature many decades to correct, our caretaker attitude has corrected in less than four years. The students carry this attitude back to their homes and cherished wilderness and now fulfill their destiny as caretakers.

5

Aloneness

I camped alone for the better part of a month. Grandfather had gone deep into the southern part of the Pine Barrens to visit an old Native American friend and Rick was away with his family for most of the summer. Certainly I had camped many times alone before, but this was the longest I had gone without seeing another person. For about the first two weeks, it was so good to be alone. I had no one to please but myself and I could practice my skills endlessly without having to discuss what should be practiced with Rick. There is also that timelessness that occurs when one is alone, for I was governed now by my own internal clock. Time becomes necessary only when other people are involved. So too was there the profound freedom that comes with the aloneness, a freedom to do whatever I wanted, whenever I wanted.

However, after the novelty of the first two weeks of aloneness wore off I began to feel very lonely. I had accomplished and witnessed so many things that I wanted to share them with someone, but there was no one there. At first the feeling of loneliness only hit me around the fire at

77

nightfall, a time when we would normally share things with each other. Then as the days passed the pangs of loneliness would become more frequent. Especially in the quiet hours after dark the loneliness became acute. I found myself doing things just to keep my mind off of my loneliness and on other things. The skills I began to practice became more involved, requiring more concentration or physical performance. So too did I find myself talking to myself out loud just to hear a human voice.

Now going well into my third week alone, I began to feel a prisoner of this aloneness. I thought frequently about going out of the woods and heading back home for a while. I even considered going to one of the closer houses just to watch people for a while. My conversations with myself were becoming rather lengthy and complicated. I even began to answer myself, frequently thinking out loud. After a while all I could think about was how alone and abandoned I felt. The loneliness saturated my every mood, to a point where I could think of nothing else at all. I so desperately wanted to share so much of what I had done over the past several weeks with someone, anyone. At this point I began to doubt myself. I thought that if I were to ever understand what Grandfather did I would have to love to be alone. Right then I hated it with a passion.

Grandfather so often told me how important extended periods of aloneness would become to my development, not only in survival but especially in the things of the spirit. Aloneness and asceticism were part of a person's spiritual teachings, and without that one could only understand part of the truth. This really bothered me, for I thought that somehow the woods and the world of spirit were trying to drive me away. They seemed to be somehow using my isolation and loneliness as a weeding device. It was like some kind of test that I had to pass. I knew that this should be an easy and much welcomed process, but the aloneness and isolation became profound loneliness. I became so disgusted with myself for feeling this way. I felt unworthy, for loneliness did not seem to be part of Grandfather's consciousness.

Finally on the first day of the fourth week I decided that I could take no more and began to pack up my camp. I would just go home for a few days and then come back to the woods after I had gotten enough company. Just as I put all of my things in my cache, I looked up with a start. Grandfather was sitting at the edge of camp watching me. At first I felt overjoyed to see him and wanted to run right over to him, but this feeling was soon supplanted by the feeling of guilt. Grandfather knew that I was to be alone for at least four weeks, in fact he had advised it, but now I was leaving early and felt very embarrassed for giving in. He kept watching me with a half smile on his face, though there was no accusation or disappointment to be found in his eyes. He said nothing, but just motioned me over to sit down.

I approached him humbly, feeling that in some way I had disgraced him and myself. Without waiting for me to ask a question he said, "I was expecting that it would be about this time when you would leave. I knew that the loneliness would eventually try to drive you from the woods." I was shocked by his statement, not only because he had known the time I would be driven from the woods, but also by what would drive me away. I told him then that I felt like I had dishonored him in some way, but I just couldn't take being alone anymore. I felt that the loneliness was getting in the way of everything else and because of the loneliness I did not feel myself worthy of a spiritual path. He then said, "There is a vast expanse between being alone and loneliness, and you must find the difference. We all must face that question someday, and yours is now." With those words he began to tell me the story of his aloneness.

Grandfather said that he had been wandering for quite a few years when he hit the tremendous barrier of loneliness. Certainly he missed his people, but he had traveled back to their encampment several times over those early years. He also encountered many people in his journeys, so his aloneness was not always that prolonged. However, there was a period in his life when he faced true aloneness for nearly ten years. It was during those years that he did not speak to or see another human. He was just too deep into the trackless wilderness of Canada, where few if any people ever ventured. In fact, during that time he rarely even found a track or any other evidence of another human. It was then, in the beginning of this long period of asceticism, that he would have to face the demon of loneliness.

Grandfather said that the loneliness and oppressive isolation did not hit him all at once. Instead it was a gradual process that overtook him slowly. At first he found that many of his questions were going unanswered. He yearned for the elders, needing their advice about many things, but he knew that there would be no way he could get to them. His feelings of being isolated and abandoned were especially intense at night, but soon they even intensified during the day. It was not so much that he missed people in general, for he had always avoided people outside of his own tribe. He just missed his family and tribe. Though, after a while, he began to long for anyone to come along, even if they were in the wilderness for the wrong reasons. The need to talk to someone became a driving passion that saturated his every waking hour.

Even with the passage of time and season, the feelings of intense loneliness never weakened. On the contrary, they grew stronger. There was never a period of relief, not even for a moment. No matter what Grandfather did, he could not shake that horrible longing. Several times he purposely moved camp, for no other reason than the change of scenery might take away the sting of isolation, but to no avail. So too did he practice skills and disciplines that would involve full concentration of thought and action, but here too he found no comfort. It came to a point where he could not think or function at all without the horrible feeling of loneliness overtaking him altogether and overshadowing everything else. He knew all along that someday he would have to face that intense loneliness, and that is what kept him going even in the deepest moments of despair.

In desperation, Grandfather began to look to nature and spirit for comfort. Even there, the communications were weak and after a while became obscure altogether. The piercing loneliness overshadowed everything and even excluded any spiritual conversation or understanding. Grandfather knew very well that he would have to transcend this loneliness or it would forever become his demon. It would defeat him unless he understood and finally defeated its smothering power. Aloneness was a vital part of any spiritual path and he had to separate aloneness from being lonely, but he had no idea as to where to begin his search for answers. What had kept him going for so long

was his sheer determination, but even that was beginning
to erode.

It was at this point, after many seasons of being absolutely
alone, that he decided to travel out of the Canadian wilderness and back to his people, or at least into areas where he
could find some old ones living alone. As he slowly packed
up camp he began to argue with himself about giving in to
the loneliness. He argued that he needed to see someone,
anyone, because this isolation was affecting his every mood
and action. On the other hand he knew how important it was
to be alone, especially for those on a spiritual path. He knew
that if not at this point in his life, then he would have to
face the demon of loneliness eventually. He lingered for
several more days in his camp area, even though he had
pulled everything down and scattered it to the earth. The
internal struggle to go or stay became overwhelming.

Finally, in a sheer act of desperation, he decided that he
would leave the area and go back to his people. He headed
south, a direction that he assumed would bring him out of
this wilderness quickly, rather than retrace his journey to
the southwest. What he did not realize was that his route
would bring him deeper into the wilderness and into the
high mountain areas, many of which had no passes leading
out. He wandered into the mountains for days before he
realized that he was walking deeper into the wilderness.
The surrounding peaks had already been covered by the first
snowfall of the season and Grandfather knew that unless he
found some mountain pass he would be trapped here for the
winter. It was far too late for him to backtrack now, so all
he could do was to search out an accessible pass.

Days slipped by as he repeatedly tried and failed to find
a mountain pass. The trails he had chosen thus far were
too high and slippery to afford safe passage. So too did the
pre-winter storms batter the higher peaks frequently and at
times he found himself wading through waist-deep snow.
Finally resolving himself to the fact that none of the trails he
had taken would lead him anywhere, he moved back down
into a small deep valley where he built a temporary camp.
What became foremost on his mind, once the necessities of
camp were taken care of, was to build a set of snowshoes.
He had only one hope of getting out and that was to make the
snowshoes so that he could get through the high mountain

snows. This was his last hope for getting out before the fury of full winter hit.

He worked feverishly on the snowshoes for several days. Proper materials were now a little more difficult to come by. He also had to build a larger pair than he normally would, with a tighter weave, such were the deep powder conditions of the higher snows. Finally after three days the snowshoes were completed and he had stored up enough food to last him well into his journey. Before dawn of the fourth day he struck out again to the mountains. Out of all the passes he had tried he knew that there was one that would hold the most hope. Though it had a bad exposure to any oncoming storm, if the weather held, he would stand the best chance. It seemed to be the easiest climb and most of the deeper snow had been swept from the rock faces by the strong winds of previous days. With prayers on his lips and hope in his heart he left camp and headed directly to the pass.

It took him nearly half the day to arrive at the base of the mountain pass. Without hesitation he decided to build a camp and spend the night. Even when he struck out the next day, the camp would be left standing in case he could not make it through the pass and was forced to retreat. At least then he would have a safe refuge to recuperate from his attempt. He also decided that attempting this pass so late in the day he might be forced to spend the night on the barren, exposed rocks high above. That would afford little protection and no way of building a shelter as the rock faces were high above timberline. Even if the conditions were absolutely perfect, it would be a difficult and treacherous climb, a climb that would easily demand much of a day. He also had no idea of what he faced on the other side. He could only guess that it led down.

In the place where he decided to put his camp there was already light snow on the ground from previous storms. He was much higher up in the mountains than he had been in the last camp and a good snowstorm would very likely dump heavy amounts on the area. He took a great deal of time to build the shelter solid and strong, designing it to withstand heavy snows on the roof. He also spent the latter part of the day gathering up firewood and making sure his hand drill worked without fail. These he would leave inside the shelter to assure that they remained dry. So too did he gather nuts, roots, and some of the last remaining berries in the area, again storing them deep in his shelter. Food would be impossible to obtain during any sort of mountain blizzard.

That night he went into the shelter early in the hopes of getting a good night's sleep. Unfortunately his sleep was racked with hideous nightmares of slipping and falling from high rocks. Several times he awoke in a cold sweat, feeling that he was in the process of falling. He dreamed of snows and blizzard conditions, of avalanches burying him, and of huge chunks of ice falling from the mountain peaks. His final awakening was to the sound of a thundering rock slide. He dreamed that he had fallen and started the slide that threatened to bury and crush him. He awoke with a sense of terror, to a point where he uncontrollably shook all over. The whole scenario of dreams shook him up so badly that he was reluctant to leave camp at first.

He gazed up the icy peaks toward the pass for a long time, watching the first glimmers of daylight begin to light the highermost spires. Now with his confidence building and what appeared to be the start of a beautiful day, he struck out from camp and headed to the pass. At first the trek was quite easy. He followed animal trails up to the base of the steeper elevations. The animal trails switched back and forth across the face of the lower mountain, making it an easy walk. However, as Grandfather reached the midpoint, the trails steepened and the snows grew deeper. Eventually he had to put on his snowshoes before he could continue any higher. From past experience, if the snow got deeper than the knee he would be using far too much energy. He had to conserve energy if he was to ever make it through the pass.

Grandfather quickly strapped on his snowshoes and proceeded without delay. The deep snows and steeper conditions made his progress slow, even with the snowshoes. At times he had to crawl and at other times he had to use sticks to help him keep his footing. Finally by high noon he was past the upper tree lines and now was facing open slopes. Eventually he reached the barren rocks that had been cleaned by the winds and he could take off his snowshoes and begin to move more quickly. His progress was slowed rather abruptly again when he found that much of the upper exposed rocks were covered in sheer ice. He had to fashion rock spikes and use these as traversing spikes to keep from slipping off the slope and over the cliff. Several times the rock spikes broke or did not hold at all, sending him sliding down several terrifying feet.

Grandfather had to pour all of his consciousness into what he was doing. He could not take his mind off the icy slopes for even a moment. Each rock spike had to be chipped solidly into the ice and each foot had to be put into a position that would not slip. One wrong move, one slight shift of weight, and he would be carried down the slope and over the cliff to his death. With all of his concentration poured into what he was doing he did not notice how long it was taking him to traverse the upper slope. At the rate he was going he would not even make it to the top of the pass by nightfall and would be forced to spend the entire night in full exposure to the elements. Nor did he notice the approach of an oncoming storm, which would certainly catch him on the icy slope if he did not pick up his speed. His concentration was so absolute that he had no other sensation than himself, the rock, and the ice.

Finally Grandfather reached a point on the slope where he could rest. There was a small indent into the side of the slope that was caused from the dislodging of a large boulder in a past season. It appeared to him to be much like a huge bird's nest or bowl, cut deep into the slope. It would afford him some flat ground, a partial buffer to the wind, and a much needed resting place. Once Grandfather was inside the boulder bowl and his concentration removed from the rock face, he began to view his surroundings. He immediately realized that he would never make it to the higher area before full dark, nor could he make a full retreat before full dark. He had two choices: proceed up the slope, climbing in the dark, or spend the night in the boulder bowl. It was then that he also noticed the oncoming storm.

Grandfather was terrified. Panic began to set in for he realized that any choice he made could mean his death. If he stayed in the rock bowl for the night he might survive, but with the oncoming storm it seemed highly unlikely. If he tried to climb across the face to the higher pass he would face climbing in the dark, a climb that was treacherous enough in full light. Even then when he eventually hit the pass he would have to weather out the oncoming storm in full exposure. The storm looked to him as if it contained an awesome power. He could already see the distant peaks being obscured by driving snow and the winds now were steadily increasing. His only hope was to try to go back down to his camp and hopefully beat the storm and fast disappearing light.

He knew that the climb down would be more perilous and difficult than the climb up, but that was the only choice he had. At least he would be part of the way down the slope when he was reached by full dark or the storm. Without fully resting, he refashioned his rock spikes and began the long journey back down. He went much slower than he had before, caused more by taking his time than by what the rock face dictated. He began to slip more frequently and placement of his feet was far more difficult, such was his reverse angle of descent. At one point along the journey his stone spikes gave way and he slid several yards down the rock face and dangerously close to the cliff. The only way he could continue with the climb was to go straight back to the rock bowl and begin over again.

It was fast approaching dusk and the winds were howling across the rock face as Grandfather finally reached the rock bowl. Again, without much of a rest, he climbed out again. He had not gone more than a few yards when he realized that he would not be able to make it back to his camp. The winds had increased so much that they threatened to tear him from the face. He now had only one choice and that was to spend the night back in the rock bowl. By the time he got back to the bowl it was full dark, the winds were raging, and now it was beginning to snow hard. Fortunately, the storm was hitting the rock bowl at a slight angle, and this gave Grandfather protection from the full onslaught of the storm. Grandfather prayed feverishly as he listened to the winds and looked out into the darkness. He was trapped and without a good shelter he knew that the chance of his survival was minimal.

The rage of the storm increased as the hours passed. Eventually Grandfather became entombed by snow in the rock bowl. At this point, he was now totally out of the wind and the insulation of the snow kept him from freezing. The hours passed by miserably, but at least he was alive. He could hear the screaming winds, even through the muffling snows, and there was no let up in their intensity. He packed at the snow around him to create a small room. Several times he had to punch his arm through the snow cover to let in fresh air. Each time he had to reach farther and farther out, as the snow's depth increased. At least now when there was a break in the weather, it would become easier to traverse the slope and head back to his camp. The snow would surely accumulate on the slope and cover the treacherous ice. Using his snowshoes, he knew that he would at least stand a better chance, and not slip as he had before.

Finally, as he punched through the snow, he could see the faint glimmer of daylight coming through the air hole, now several feet above him. Though the storm still raged outside, he knew that he could not stay in the small snow cave much longer. His energy was depleted and he had begun to shiver intermittently through the night. Freezing to death would not be far away and he would have to move as soon as possible. He punched his way through the wall of his little snow cave and into stormy daylight. The landscape had been transformed and deep snow now clung to the slopes, completely covering the ice. As he gazed out onto the barren landscape, he saw no break in the storm and without hesitation he put on his snowshoes and carefully left the snow cave.

Very cautiously and slowly he began to work his way across the snowy slope. Now, with the aid of the snowshoes on the deep snow he could almost walk upright, so unlike the belly-down crawl of the day before. For a moment it passed through his mind that he should try now to make it to the pass, but the storm's fury put it forever out of the question. Instead he continued relentlessly, concentrating on every move, the feel of the snow, and the lay of the slope. In several of the steeper areas he saw that he was climbing directly beneath an avalanche and had to use even more care in his foot placement. One small avalanche gave in behind him and narrowly missed wiping him off the face of the mountain. The cold also bit deep into his flesh to a point where he could barely feel his hands or feet. It now took all of his concentration just to keep going on.

He began to draw on a strength he did not know he had. His body and mind felt so in tune with the mountain and snow, to a point where movement became almost effortless. Soon the power of the storm was forgotten as he began to make greater progress. He could feel his body living on the edge of life and death, traveling as gracefully as a well-conditioned animal. He loved the feeling, for he became totally focused on its power and motion. It became as a dance, more fluid than he had ever known. At this point he no longer felt the cold and he began to sweat, even though the storm kept up its raging intensity. He felt so proud of himself, for the years of training had truly snatched him from the perilous edge of death.

It was not long before Grandfather reached his camp. In a short period of time he had dug out his shelter and had a warming fire going inside. He cooked and ate some of his food, then melted snow for drinking water. He could feel his full strength returning as he fell into a state of deep peace. He felt so alive and whole that he began to laugh and cry at the same time. Something on that mountain had profoundly moved something inside of him but he did not know what it was. All he knew was that something had changed and he liked the feeling. He had not felt this much peace and serenity in a very long time. He reveled in the moment to a point where he felt like he was going to burst with uncontrollable joy. He had gained a passion for living like he had never known. It wasn't long before Grandfather fell into a deep and much needed sleep.

Grandfather awoke the next morning to a beautiful day. The sun shone down bright and the air was pure and still. He could feel the warmth of the sun and could go about his morning chores without his robe. The feeling of elation that he had the day before made his day even brighter and he sang as he worked. He still could not understand what had shifted inside of him or even how it had gotten there. He wondered if it had been the fact that he had been so close to the edge of death but had beaten it back and robbed it of its triumph. Many times, after walking the edge of life and death, Grandfather would experience a similar elation, but this was not quite the same. This was something far different than one gets from the high achievement when triumphing over impossible odds, but he could not yet understand.

As Grandfather sat down to take in all of the beauty that surrounded him, the answer suddenly came to him. He was not lonely anymore. He still did not know why it had happened, but the change in him was transcending the loneliness that had haunted him for so many months. In fact, he had not been lonely since he decided to make the climb to the pass. He began to wonder if the loneliness was yet to come back. Certainly his full attention was on his treacherous trek and there had been no room for loneliness, or for that matter anything else. His concentration had been so absolute that there could be nothing else. But he somehow knew that the loneliness would not return, or at least not as it had before. There was too much peace within him and he enjoyed the solitude. There was not even a longing to go back to his people, as had been before. Even though he would like to see them, he didn't need to see them.

He began to think deeply about the change in himself and why it might have happened. It was then when he remembered what Great-grandfather Coyote Thunder had told him about being alone and loneliness. He had said, "The chasm between being alone and loneliness is deep. The way you begin to be alone and at peace without being lonely is to know that you are with your best friend. When you are at peace with yourself and love yourself, you can never be lonely. Only when one learns to love himself can he love another. You must find that love for yourself before you can touch the purity of aloneness. Love of self, without being selfish, will not allow loneliness to exist. Love of self also creates a love for everything else and brings us closer to the sacred oneness."

Grandfather thought long and hard about Coyote Thunder's words, trying to fit them into what had happened to him on the face of the mountain. As Grandfather retraced all the events of the past several days, it finally occurred to him what had happened to change loneliness into aloneness. It was at the point when he was making the journey back to camp that he began to appreciate what his body could do. In that appreciation he also found a love for himself. It was at this point when he stopped being critical of his every thought and action and began to accept himself, value himself, as he would everyone and everything else. That is when his journey became an effortless dance and he felt so much a part of the mountain and snow. That is when the loneliness vanished forever.

Grandfather's story of aloneness helped me through the next several weeks. Though I cannot say there weren't periods of time when I felt lonely, for there were, they were not as severe. Nor did the periods of loneliness get to a point where I wanted to leave the Pine Barrens. I did begin to grow more comfortable with my aloneness because I began to like being with myself. I stopped being so critical of my actions and began to enjoy my mistakes and failures. As Grandfather had said, you can't be lonely when you are with your best friend, yourself. So too did I learn that spiritually one can never be alone. We are all connected to all other entities of the earth through the-spirit-that-moves-through-all-things, and once realizing that spirit we become one with all things. There can be no loneliness.

6

White Death

Grandfather did not have much if any contact with the white culture in his youth. Slowly, through the years of his travels he began to encounter more and more of the white man. He did not despise the white race, only their way of thinking. It was contrary to everything he believed in and most of all contradictory to the laws of creation. He could find no real truth in the life-style of these people. All he found was a culture that chased the false gods of the flesh and destroyed everything in their path. He saw a culture that killed its grandchildren to feed its children, a culture that made decisions for the satisfaction and convenience of the flesh today, and threw away tomorrow, decisions that would one day destroy the earth. Again, it was not the white race that Grandfather so loathed, but their way of thinking and living, which is the thinking of the global society today.

I remember when I was still quite young, hearing Grandfather talk of the white race with a tone of hatred in his voice. It bothered me deeply for the first few months that I was with him. He held the white race in contempt, and I was white, so I began to think that he hated me too. I often wondered what he really felt about me, but was afraid to ask. I guess that I really didn't want to know. Anytime he said something about the white race, I held myself as responsible as the entire race itself, as if I were one of the causes of his anger. I felt very guilty at times, especially when we encountered destruction, dumping, or polluting. This tended to get very confusing for me, for he never said anything about my being part of it all. He treated me much like a loving grandfather would treat his grandson, yet I still felt responsible for the sins of the white race.

As the first few months went by and we encountered more and more destruction, this question of how Grandfather felt about me began to weigh very heavy on my thoughts. The guilt that I felt became very profound at times. Every time I heard Grandfather speak of the destruction and ignorance of the white race I would drift into a depression that would sometimes last for several days. I just could not understand the contradiction of how Grandfather could despise a culture of people and not hate me at the same time. After all, I was part of it all. I lived in a house, rode in cars, and went to school, like everyone else. Was not I also as responsible as everyone else? I just could not understand how Grandfather could make any separation between everyone else and me. Finally, unable to bear the confusion and guilt anymore, I asked Grandfather how he felt about me.

We had been on a short hike away from the Medicine Cabin when we came upon a huge illegal dumping ground. We had been to the area not two months before and the area was as pristine and untouched as any natural area of the Pine Barrens. In fact, we had camped near a small stream and had freely drank from the waters without fear. Now it lay in ruin. Stretching before us lay all manner of debris, from household goods, to old paint cans, twisted metal, rotting food, cans, bottles, and drums of old motor oil. The stream now was choked with litter, vile, and contaminated with a slick of iridescent oil. Many trees had been randomly cut and left where they lay to make room for the trucks to turn around. Everywhere was the stench of rotted garbage and the caustic smell of undefined chemicals.

Grandfather stood at the edge of all of this destruction and cried. I was horrified beyond words. I could see the look of pain on Grandfather's face. It was the look generated by severe loss mingled with hatred. I know that he could not comprehend this kind of destruction, for it was far beyond his way of thinking. It was as if someone had wantonly killed his mother. Grandfather damned the white race with a seething anger, an anger that Grandfather rarely showed. He turned to me and said in a trembling voice, "You see, this is caused by stupidity. These people think that they can live above and beyond the laws of creation. They destroy land and feel no remorse. They destroy the land because of their lust and greed. They care nothing of the land or tomorrow."

I was overwhelmed with guilt and simply told Grandfather, without thinking, that I was sorry. Grandfather looked at me and asked, "What do you have to be sorry for? You are not one of these people." I then told Grandfather of my plight. I said that I live much the same way as these people do and that I am part of the white man's culture. I told him that I am white, not Native American, and thus part of this destruction. I told him that I could not understand how he could hate the white man's destruction and not hate me also. I also said that I did not understand what he meant, my not being one of these people. A look of concern came over his face, for he must now have realized that I did not understand and could not make the conscious separation between me and the white man.

He smiled at me lovingly and said, "I do not hate the white man, grandson, just his way of thinking and living. You are not a white man, but a child of the earth. Skin color and blood do not make you a child of the earth. It is your heart and your beliefs that make you one with all things. I do not condemn or curse the white race, only their ignorance and destruction. They know no better. They are not my enemies, but their ways are. I never considered you part of that way of thinking, for your heart has always beat as one with the earth. I hate no one, not even my enemies. I only hate the ignorance of these people and that is what I curse. It is their ignorance that I will fight, not the people. Not every white man destroys the earth as not every Native American protects the earth. No race is responsible, but we are all responsible for ignorance."

Grandfather went on to explain to me that he did not always think that way. There was a time in his life when he blamed all the white race for destroying the earth, and hated them all. He told me that he had carried this hatred for many years of his wandering. He saw no good in the white culture. The same culture that was destroying the earth had also destroyed many tribes and people of the earth. He had seen the imprisonment of all tribes, the starvation, and the living conditions that were worse than any of white man's animals could ever bear. Though he hated the white man, he saw no use in fighting against them, for their numbers were too strong. Many of his people had died in the past and a true warrior was always the last to pick up the lance. Instead of confrontation, Grandfather just chose to avoid the white man at all costs. He did not even think that they could be taught the old ways, far less listen to what he had to say.

He told me that all of that hatred changed and refocused at one point in his life, where he no longer hated the white race but only their way of thinking. It was in the first ten years of his wandering that this metamorphosis took place and he finally found in his heart a love for the white man. His early years of wandering had taken him into many different parts of the country and deep into vast new wilderness areas. Many times, in order to get to certain areas, Grandfather had to pass dangerously close to white civilizations. He feared for his life and he knew that if he were caught he would eventually be imprisoned on a reservation. That is why he always sought to travel in the deepest and most inaccessible reaches of the wilderness. It would be highly unlikely that any white man would be there.

So too was his stealth as a hunter and scout far superior to that of the white man. He could exist where others would die and he could become invisible to anyone who tried to find him. He needed nothing of the outside world, thus it became easy for him to avoid the white culture. Even to those trappers who sometimes wandered the wilderness alone, he found no contest. They were just barely better off than their white brothers of the cities and towns. They could never be part of the land, for their life and thinking kept them removed from that oneness. They were aliens and did not belong on the earth. To Grandfather, their survival skills were inept and their existence in wilderness was a joke. Even those who removed themselves from the white culture to make a living from the wilderness still needed the tools of white society to survive.

In his travels, though rarely, Grandfather would secretly observe the activities of small towns and villages. He would prowl the limits, just outside the sight of man and animals, observing the commotion that went on. He would listen to conversations, watch people's walks, observe how aware they were of their surroundings, and look into their faces for clues to their happiness. Though he detested the stench and commotion of these places, he knew that he needed to learn what they taught firsthand. His skills as a scout enabled him to easily travel within the confines of any town and avoid detection. He could easily become invisible to animals so escaping man's detection was effortless. He wanted to know what drove the white race to this insanity, to this destruction. He wanted to comprehend the consciousness of that alien society in its fullest. That way, by knowing why, he might be able to come up with a way of reeducating them.

The more Grandfather observed the workings of the white race, the more he detested them. He could see no way of reaching them with the truth. To him, they were a lost cause. They were nothing more than a group of encapsulated, unhappy people, unaware of themselves, the world around them, or each other. They did not even know they were unhappy. It seemed to Grandfather that a man's happiness, his success, in this society was based on external possessions and little else. These people seemed to fret, to strive, and to slave, with little other purpose in their lives than to make things more convenient. They looked upon the wilderness as a hostile environment, something that should be avoided at all costs. White man tried to insulate himself from the life-giving forces of the earth, to remove himself, and to control his environment. In this society, it is a constant battle between man and nature. White man wanted to rise above all laws of creation and bring it under his complete control.

Grandfather never went near the larger towns. Instead he kept to the smaller hamlets. Even from a distance big towns were more than Grandfather could handle. He had no idea that there were even bigger towns, called cities. So in his early days of exploring the white man's civilization, he stayed to the small hamlets and homesteads. There was always enough going on in them to satisfy his curiosity. Even in these small places, he was appalled at the waste, at the way man farmed and kept his animals, and at the conditions that the white man chose to live under. He could not imagine that there could be anything worse, that was until he took his first journey toward the east and encountered a city the white man called Chicago.

Grandfather had been wandering over the prairie country, through what he learned the white man called Iowa. He had been wandering toward the east for days, avoiding towns and homesteads along the way. He could not understand the numerous fence rows that he encountered along the way. And with each passing day, the fence rows and cultivated fields became more numerous. He was appalled at the fact that buffalo had once freely roamed these prairies and now were all but gone. Gone too were the Native Americans who once roamed these prairies. Now the prairies themselves were disappearing to the fields and fence rows of man. Cattle now roamed in place of the buffalo, and this saddened Grandfather. He remembered stories about the buffalo of the plains and how the herds were so large that they stretched from horizon to horizon. Now all was gone to the greed of the white man.

As Grandfather continued his eastward trek, called more by inner vision than by mindful purpose, he began to see more and more signs of modern civilization. It became more and more difficult to avoid the farms and towns of man. Eventually, Grandfather was compelled to travel at night, to remain undetected. After a while, that even became a difficult task. He had to take great care as to where he set his camp for fear of being located when he was asleep during the day. Still he was driven onward, but now by a force that he could only define as spirit. He knew that he had to continue his journey, but he did not understand why. He was now far removed from his natural element, in the fields of society, almost like being behind enemy lines in his mind. Here, he felt like an alien.

Midway through what started out as his typical night travel, Grandfather began to hear strange noises in the distance, sounds that he had never before heard. Looking toward the east he saw an eerie glow in the sky, the color and texture he had never before witnessed in nature. Often, the wind would change direction and he would catch a terrible stench that at times would make him sick to his stomach. As he moved on, all of this strangeness intensified until a point where he was absolutely terrified. He did not know its source, whether man or spirit, and decided to camp where he was and await full light before he went on. He hardly slept the rest of the night, being awakened frequently by the stench, the strange sounds, and the lights in the sky. It was just before dawn when Grandfather finally fell into a deep sleep.

He was awakened by strange noises and the distant voices of people. Cautiously he looked up from where he had fallen asleep. To his shock, he had fallen asleep on a small tree-lined hill, overlooking a road. On the road, a horse and wagon were going by, loaded with several pigs. The driver and his passenger were talking loudly, so as to be heard over the creak and rattle of the wagon on the bumpy road. Grandfather laid close to the ground, fearing that he might have been seen. He waited for a long time before he put his head up again, and only after he was sure that the wagon was well away from the area. He looked again, up and down the road, but there was no other evidence of people coming. However, he could see by the wear marks in the dirt that the road was heavily used and he was sure that there would be more people coming along at any time.

He slowly arose from his open bed and to his horror, the hill was right between two roadways. All around him and stretching for miles was nothing more than rolling hills and short grasses. There were only a few islands of deep vegetation. During the wanderings of the previous night it had not occurred to him that he was traveling right out in the open. The small rolling hills had given him a deceptive sense of security in darkness, but now he realized how vulnerable he was. He could be easily seen from any direction, and he began to feel like a cornered animal. Scanning the area around the hill, he saw people working in the various fields, preventing him from backtracking. Before him lay the road and beyond the road was a small homestead. He could clearly see that in the distance was a small town. There was no way he could escape, at least not until darkness.

He cautiously laid back down and carefully buried himself
in the fallen leaves. Unless someone walked right on him,
he would be safe. For hours he lay motionless, as he heard
numerous wagons pass and more people talking. Near the
middle of the day, all travel seemed to stop, and he could
hear no sound coming from any direction. He cautiously
lifted his head from the ground to get a look at the area
again. No one was around and nothing was moving. People
had seemed to disappear from the face of the earth. As he
scanned the immediate area, he lifted his eyes to the distant
eastern horizon. From his perch on the small hill he could
barely make out the outline of a distant mountain range, but
it was nothing like any range he had ever seen. It seemed to
rise out of the plains like a wall, terminating the wilderness
in all manner of geometric forms that defied anything the
Creator would make.

He scrutinized the distant mountains, trying to understand
them, when to his amazement he spied several columns of
smoke arising from the peaks. At first he thought that the
smoke was from campfires, but it was far too much smoke
to be from a camp. He then thought it could be from a brush
or forest fire, but the smoke columns did not travel over the
ground. He was mesmerized by the distant range, trying
desperately in his mind to figure out what it was all about.
It was then that he saw the numerous roads that lay before
the cliffs, and the movement of wagons and people along
those roads. To his horror, he realized that he was looking
at one of the white man's great cities. He had never seen one
before and had only heard about them from various people
he encountered in his travels. This was more than he could
bear and all he could do was to stare at the city, terrified.

He was paralyzed with this fear. He could not imagine
something so immense that it would appear as a mountain
range from the distance. He gazed at the thick blanket of
smoke that hung above the city and he could not understand
how those people could live in such conditions. He waited
at the crest of the hill for hours trying to comprehend the
vastness of what he observed. He wondered if it could in
fact be some sort of hallucination, for there was nothing
he had encountered in the past that would even compare to
this. His fear was laced, however, with a certain fascination
and he wondered if the spirit world had not led him to this

point to observe this city. After all, he had no idea why he had wandered so far to the east, other than it had felt like he had been compelled to do so.

As the sun began to set and the lights of the city began to make the clouds of smoke above glow with an eerie light, Grandfather began to scan the landscape leading to the city. In the last remaining light, he began to plan how he would reach the city unobserved. As usual, he waited until full dark before he moved. He had the entire journey mapped out in his mind. He knew how long it would take him to get there and back, where there were safe hiding places along the way, and where all the probable escape routes were. He knew if he were caught in the area he would probably be taken to a reservation, or possibly even killed. He had to be extremely careful. His fear was now set aside and curiosity began to guide him, though deep inside his apprehension was intense.

The journey began with relative ease. He stayed to the landscapes that held the most brush and cover. When crossing a road, he was careful not to leave any tracks, which was not very difficult to do. From his experience, he doubted if anyone here could track him, or for that matter see tracks at all. He knew that some of the mountain men that he had encountered could track, but not very well to say the least. His trip took far longer than he had expected, and he covered only about half the distance that he should have. Most of the reason for the slow travel was that he had to take great care in his movements, taking no chances of being seen. The trip would have gone much faster if he did not have to worry about being caught. He began to realize that he would just barely make it to the city before first light. There would be no way he could make it back to the hill by the next morning.

As he approached the city limits, the first thing on his mind was to find a place to spend the day without being seen. It was so difficult to get within the limits of the city. Huge garbage dumps and choking air made any real progress painful. Even during this early hour, there were many people about, but Grandfather suspected that these must be ones without homes, such were their actions. To him, they appeared to be no better off than the rats that fed in the dumps. At least the rats seemed to have a place to live.

These poor souls just slept in the streets, under buildings, or in the doorways of buildings. They appeared battered and lonely, victims of a society that did not work for them. He was appalled at the general conditions of the city and it sickened him to be so close. It was horrifying for him to realize that he would have to spend an entire day enveloped in this insanity and stench.

He searched around the outskirts of the city, looking for a place to spend the day without being seen. Now he had to take great care in his movements, for now he saw many more people wandering or sleeping on the streets. He clung to the shadows and piles of nameless debris that covered the street. Several times he had to slip by a sleeping tramp, but he began to realize after a while that these people seemed to have very little awareness. His travel became easier as he realized that he had very little chance of being seen. Finally, as the first glimmers of daylight began to appear, he located a place to spend the day. It was a raised wooden platform with wooden planks for sides, appearing much like a pen. He knew that if he could get inside the platform he would have a clear view of the city street and yet remain out of sight.

He crept up to the platform, deftly sticking close to the shadows. A man sat on a chair, just outside the door that led to the platform. Grandfather could see the man was wearing a gun and an unmistakable uniform, probably a soldier or a sheriff of sorts. It took him almost to full daylight before he reached the outskirts of the platform and crawled under. Luckily there was a side plank that had come away from the post and it gave him just enough room to get inside. Once inside the sanctuary of the platform, he breathed a sigh of relief, finally feeling somewhat secure after hours of torment. He did not move at first, but relaxed to compose himself and listen for any sounds that could be a threat. After all, the guard now sat just above him on the platform. Grandfather worried that the stench of the city would make him cough and alert the guard.

As the first shafts of daylight filtered through the cracks of the boards, Grandfather got his first full look at the inside of the platform. At one end there was a pile of old boards, bits of twisted metal, and broken glass. On the distant wall were the remnants of an old trapdoor, now wired shut, that would have at one time given an easy access to the underside of the platform. Strewn randomly against all the walls of the platform were piles of garbage, mostly paper and dead plants that had attempted to grow in the sterility of the soil. To Grandfather's horror, imprinted in the dirt were evidence of human tracks, hand and knee prints, and several definite outlines left by a sleeping person. He suddenly realized that this area was also probably used by one of the tramps he had encountered when he reached the city limits. However, now it seemed to be abandoned because the tracks were many days old.

Grandfather began to move deeper into the platform when he heard the guard move above. He froze his action and listened to him walk back and forth several times, stopping here and there to look around. Suddenly, Grandfather heard a cough coming from the other side of the old lumber pile and the guard jumped from the platform and moved to the old door. Grandfather lay close to the ground and slid close to the darkest wall and covered himself in bits of garbage. The guard began to call out through the slats in an angry voice. Grandfather could not understand the language, but he knew that the man was angry. Instantly, there was an abrupt stirring sound coming from the pile of old wood and in a flash a young man jumped the pile, crawled quickly across the floor, and began to move toward the other side of the platform. The guard hurried around the outside to the side the young man had headed for.

Without thinking, Grandfather grabbed the young man by the arm and put his hand to his mouth, indicating silence. The young man looked at Grandfather in terrified amazement, but obeyed without question, probably more out of fear of Grandfather than out of will. Grandfather then picked up a small block of wood and tossed it against the distant side of the platform. The guard responded by running to the other side with a demanding scream. The guard listened for a moment and then thinking that who ever had been under the platform had escaped, ran down the street, thinking that he was chasing the trespasser. Grandfather smiled at the young man and the man gave Grandfather a half-hearted reserved smile, still appearing very frightened.

Grandfather and the young tramp eyed each other for a long moment. The young man looked like he was torn between running away and staying. His curiosity getting the better of him, the young man asked Grandfather his name, but Grandfather did not understand. Seeing immediately that Grandfather did not understand his language, the young man pointed at himself and said "Paul," then pointed back to Grandfather. Grandfather, now realizing what the young man was trying to convey, pointed at himself and said his name. The young man did well with the difficult pronunciation of Grandfather's name and they both laughed silently. They spent the better part of the morning trying to communicate with each other. By early afternoon, language no longer seemed a barrier and they became immediate friends.

It did not take long before Paul realized that Grandfather wanted to learn of life in the city. Paul realized that it was more to satisfy Grandfather's curiosity than wanting to live in the city. For the next several months, Paul began to show Grandfather his world. Most of their journeys were taken at night so that they could easily travel without being seen. Grandfather saw the factories, slaughterhouses, houses, slums, and roadways. He was appalled at the thought that people were starving in the streets while others seemed to have everything they wanted. He found that there was no real brotherhood between these people of the city. Everyone seemed to be so self-absorbed in their senseless rushing, fretting, striving, and slaving for unseen riches. They seemed to live to work.

He could not understand what drove these people. How could they live so far removed from the earth and its life-giving forces? They seemed to be imprisoned, not only by the sterile walls of the city, but by their own flesh. It seemed to Grandfather that these people believed only in the flesh, and the flesh became their only god. The only ones who seemed close to being real and alive to Grandfather were those people like Paul, who lived in the streets a free life. Yet there was no freedom for them, for they were slaves to the trash heaps and imprisoned by the city. He knew that they would surely perish in the wilderness. Yet there was a camaraderie that began to build between Grandfather and these tramps. The friendship between he and Paul began to grow strong as the weeks passed, to a point where they became inseparable.

As Paul began to show Grandfather the ways of the city, Grandfather began to show Paul his ways. He began to integrate his wilderness skills to the wilderness of the city. He taught Paul and many others how to build fine warm shelters, hidden from the eyes of others. He taught them how to hunt and trap outside the city limits and showed them many edible and medicinal wild plants. He taught them to use stalking to evade their enemy and move freely about the city, and he taught them to read tracks of both man and animals. Most of all, Grandfather began to teach Paul and his friends the philosophy of wilderness. He told them of ultimate freedom from all that bound people to the city, and he explained to them that they could go back and live in perfect balance and harmony with the earth.

There began to form at the outskirts of the city a small village of people, comprised of Paul, Grandfather, and an assortment of tramps and derelicts. Grandfather became the unofficial leader, for it was he who showed them how to free themselves of the garbage piles and cold streets. Little by little, Grandfather began to wean these people from the city altogether. It was rare that they would need anything from the streets, yet the people had no idea that they were depending less and less on the city. They had no idea of Grandfather's master plan, but they trusted him like a kind old father figure. Their little village was so well hidden and protected that it was never found. Even after the addition of a large hidden lodge that would be used for meetings and teaching, the camp remained invisible.

Slowly, the little village became a tribal society. People began to work together for the good of the tribe and as always, the preservation of the earth, now their home, was the most important. Late in the summer, The Council, as the tribe now called itself, decided to move the camp farther up north and deeper into the woods. They knew that the winters would be cold and they needed the protection of the woods from the storms and from the eyes of the city dwellers. It was a slow process, because the camp had to be moved during the night, and in stages. The northern camp had to be mostly built and livable before the entire tribe could move. Colder weather was coming in fast and they had to be assured of good warm shelters at both locations. Finally, by mid-fall everyone was living in the northern camp. The old camp was scattered and abandoned so as to disappear back into the earth. There remained no evidence of the camp's existence.

The Council found that it was far easier to live in the northern camp than in the old location. They could freely move about in the day, food was more plentiful, and people grew strong and healthy. Throughout the cold winter, everyone was comfortable and well fed, thanks to Grandfather's teaching and ability to store food away. Here people began to work together even more. They no longer relied on finding discarded clothing in the city but began to make their own. In fact, it was rare now that they would ever use things that were manufactured. Instead they preferred to make everything themselves. So too did their understanding of the philosophy of living with the earth grow strong. It was not long before they truly became children of the earth and began to despise the ways of their white brethren.

Grandfather continued to teach these people throughout the entire winter and into the next spring. They learned quickly, not only the skills of survival, tracking, and awareness, but also the spiritual teachings. They seemed to hunger for the wisdom of the spirit more than anything else, and Grandfather willingly filled the void. Grandfather had never met a group of more enthusiastic people. Certainly he had tried to teach his skills many times before, but most times he had been met with a mild disinterest. These people had tasted the insanity and prisons of the city and now hated that way of thinking and living. They wanted the riches of freedom and purity. Many would have rather died than go back to the way their lives used to be. Now the only time any would return to the city was when they were looking for others to come and live in the Council Tribe.

By midsummer, the northern camp had grown to almost three times the size as when it started. Now many of the original people were teaching the new arrivals, passing down the knowledge of survival and spirit that Grandfather had taught. Grandfather had not only become a legend here in the village, but also in the streets of the city where hobo communities existed. It became obvious to Grandfather that because the tribe's existence was becoming known and because the size of the village had expanded, that they would have to move farther north and deeper into the wilderness.

He was also feeling the calling of the spirits again and knew that it would be soon time for him to move on too. With that thought, there grew a great pain in Grandfather's heart for these people, who lived like the people of his own tribe.

Grandfather went with Paul far into the north country to scout out potential camp locations. Finally after several days of travel, they came upon an ideal location. Grandfather would now be sure that the people would do well in this place and forever stay out of range of the white man. These people were now more Indian than white, and Grandfather knew that they could very well face the dangers that any child of the earth faces. It was on the way back to the main camp that Grandfather told Paul of his plan to leave. Both cried and held each other for a very long time. They had not only become friends, but brothers, in the truest sense of the word. They knew that the separation would be very painful. Grandfather told Paul that he did not think that he could ever love a white man and Paul said that he never thought he could love an Indian. They both laughed well into the night and cried tears of joy and pain.

Grandfather remained at the main camp for several days as people packed up and prepared to move north. Finally on the last night together, the people held a feast in Grandfather's honor, and to honor the first child born to the tribe. Grandfather felt so at peace and so satisfied. Not only was everything eaten taken from the earth, but no tools of the white man were seen. Only some of the new arrivals had on remnants of white man's clothing, but Grandfather knew that it would not be long before even those things were abandoned. They feasted well into the night, finishing with a tremendous pipe ceremony where all participated. There was dancing and singing, and the night air reverberated with laughter and shouts of joy.

Grandfather was gone before first light, saying good-bye to no one, as was his way. He did not believe in separation, for in the spirit world there can be no separation, thus the term good-bye is a lie. As Grandfather sat on a high hill watching the camp moving north, he was struck with a great sense of loneliness and loss. He felt the same love for these people as he did his own. They were his tribe now and he would miss them. He finally understood that it was not the white man that he hated, but the white man's ways, his thinking, and the way he destroyed the earth. He loved these people of his new tribe and knew without a doubt that they were children of the earth. He finally understood that it was not the color of the skin that made a person one with the earth, but what was in his heart. At once Grandfather realized that all people were truly his brothers and sisters, and he had to love them.

After hearing Grandfather's story of the Council Tribe, I too could finally find peace. I now understood that when Grandfather cursed the white man, it was not the man but the consciousness of society he was cursing consciousness that could be lived by anyone who chose to remove themselves from the earth. I also learned that Grandfather loved everyone, even his enemies. He could have easily not bothered teaching those vagabonds and derelicts, but out of love for them and for the earth, he chose to stay with them and teach as much as he could. I only hoped then that I could find the love of people that Grandfather possessed.

What became very apparent to me was the fact that once the skills of the wilderness were learned, man could regain his self-respect and take charge of his destiny. It was not the color, race, religion, or economic status of a man that took him away from the earth, but a way of thinking. There are those in every society that turn their backs to the earth, not because of choice so much, but by ignorance and greed. Good or bad, I had to love them all, even those who would otherwise destroy the earth. Wars and hatred will never change anyone or anything, but adds power unto itself. Only through love for all people can we ever hope to make a difference, but first there must be love.

7

First Pilgrimage to South America

In our early days together, Rick and I had no comprehension of how far Grandfather had traveled in his life. We were amazed so often. When we asked Grandfather where he had learned a particular skill or technique, more times than not, Grandfather would tell us that the origin of the skill came not only from Mexico, Canada, Alaska, or even Central America. His knowledge and collection of skills came from the peoples of the United States but seemed to reach far outside the borders. Frequently, Grandfather would include with his description of a certain skill its origins and how and where he had first learned its making and use. Many times, that was our only indication of how extensively Grandfather had traveled and gave us an idea as to how many people he had sought out for the skills.

We found out about his trip into the Amazon jungles quite by accident. We had assumed, since the subject had never come up, that Grandfather had never visited South America. We just figured that he had remained mostly in North America, venturing down only as far as Panama. After all, most of the skills we had learned up until this point in our lives were from the United States, and only a few had come from south of the border. On this particular occasion, we had been practicing our skill with the bow and arrow, focusing our attention on mainly aerial shots. We were trying to master the technique of hunting birds in flight or perched high in trees, but our accuracy had not been very good. We never seemed to be able to loft the arrow high enough or with enough force to hit the targets we had placed in the trees. There seemed to be something missing in our technique. Our little bows just did not seem stable enough.

Grandfather had been watching our limited ability from afar. As soon as we saw him watching, we got worse. Because I felt like I was being closely scrutinized by Grandfather, my hands began to tremble even more than they did in the earlier practice, and I began to horribly miss the shots. I just could not get any stability. As Rick took his turn and shot a few arrows, I watched Grandfather disappear inside his shelter and emerge carrying, what I assumed to be, a long stick. As he drew closer, I realized that what he was carrying was in fact a rather long bow, longer than I had ever seen. The bow was brightly colored, and two large green feathers and a small red one hung from one end. So too were the arrows brightly colored and very long. They were of a fletch design I had never before seen.

Grandfather approached us with a smile on his face. Rick and I stood gaping at the long bow as Grandfather began to string it and test its pull. The bow was majestic, the pull strong, but it lacked any abrupt curve such as was found in the "eared" or "recurved" bow that we had made so often. Instead, the bow was just one long and elegant curve. Without a word, Grandfather nocked an arrow, pulled the bow strong and steady, then released the arrow right through the same target we had been trying to hit all day. He did this twice more, until he offered the bow to us. Without awaiting any explanation, I nocked the arrow, aimed to the high target, and released the arrow. The bow was absolutely stable and true and I hit the target. Without a word, Rick did the same, also hitting the target. We were both amazed at how well the bow performed.

We asked Grandfather about the long bow, telling him that we were amazed at how well it shot and how very stable it was. Grandfather told us that the people who had shown him the bow did most of their hunting up in the trees. The bow had been designed for high shots, where the targets were relatively small and they needed stability and strength of bow draw to reach their target with any accuracy. He then told us that most of their targets were parrots and monkeys, found high up in the upper parts of the South American jungles. We were flabbergasted by what Grandfather was telling us. The jungle was always an intriguing dream to us and we wanted to have Grandfather tell us all about what it was like to go there. We had never thought to ask him if he had ever been there, and now we felt foolish that we hadn't asked. That night at the campfire, Grandfather told us of his first trip into South America.

Grandfather told us that it was more by an unconscious accident than by choice that he ended up in South America. At the time he had been traveling slowly through southern Mexico when the urge hit him to travel farther south. Up until this point in his life, he had never been farther south than the Panamanian jungles, but he just knew that the spirit was leading him farther south than that now. Stories of the immense South American jungle wilderness had only been conveyed to him in the stories that his great-grandfather, Coyote Thunder, had told him. And even these stories had been passed down to his Great-grandfather. As far as Grandfather knew, no one in his tribe had ever ventured much past the southern borders of Mexico. He was the first to go beyond.

A few years before, Grandfather had been living in the Everglades for several months and had some knowledge of tropical conditions, but nothing would compare or prepare him for what he had yet to encounter. Traveling the many jungles he had to pass through along the way proved difficult enough. He was not at all familiar with the plants and animals of these jungles and had to rely on his inner vision to guide him to what was edible and what was not. Fortunately his hunting and fishing skills proved more than adequate to obtain game, so it was rare that he was ever without meat. His plant diet, however, was severely lacking and encountering the plants he was familiar with became rarer the farther south he traveled.

By the time he reached the great South American jungles, he was rather thin and worn out from lack of a balanced diet. His drive to reach the jungle had overshadowed his common sense. He realized that he should not have been in a rush to get there and should have taken better care of his physical needs. Now that he had reached the infinite jungle, he was in rather poor condition and totally out of his element. Though he could still easily hunt and trap game, there were very few plants he was familiar with. These were also few and far between. There was no doubt in his mind that he would have to find a better diet, and get back to a healthier state of existence, before he could ever think of striking out into the deeper jungles.

Grandfather's exhaustion ran very deep. He had hardly stopped for many thousands of miles. Not once did he camp for more than a day in any area since he left the southern border of Mexico. Many times he traveled days without food, and rarely did he get a full night's sleep. The nagging spirit within seemed to drag him onward without letup. At times it would hardly let him sleep at all. Even his dreams were of the journey to the jungle, and they too had a sense of rushing. He had been definitely driven to this place, driven to the brink of utter exhaustion and malnutrition. He knew that he could not go on until he got a long period of rest and rebuilt his strength. He resolved to himself, despite the spiritual nagging, that he would stay where he was for several days before going on.

Within the span of a full day, Grandfather had built his shelter, laid out traps, built a fire, and set about making the camp comfortable. He found water easily and put up several days of meat he had hunted. Still, he lacked the vegetarian part of his diet. He had exhausted the last few familiar plants that he knew to be edible, but refused to take them all for fear of wiping out the species in the area. Eventually he lost his appetite and soon began to grow very lethargic and sickly. He could not communicate with his inner vision, eventually growing not to trust its judgment. It was only through his inner vision that he could discern the edible plants from the poisonous, and now it seemed to be failing him. The last two plants that Grandfather was guided to through his inner vision made him sick. He assumed that in his weakened state, his inner vision was rendered ineffective.

This sickness and the weakened state grew worse as the days passed. Certainly he was getting enough sleep and enough water, but his diet was sorely lacking. He began to wonder if in fact he had contracted some rare jungle disease and that was the reason for his sickness. Yet he had gone for many months of his life on strictly meat diets, especially when he was living with the Eskimo people, and he could not understand now why the lack of plants in his diet could cause such a severe reaction. He began to think seriously about making a retreat to the coast, where he knew that he could find plants he was familiar with. He thought of traveling down the Amazon River and to the delta region that he so often heard stories about. There he knew would be native people living on the fringe of the jungle. Possibly they could help him with his sickness.

It was well into his second week in the deep jungle that Grandfather decided to pack up his camp and make the journey to the coast. He knew that in his weakened state it would be very difficult at best, and he began to doubt if he would make it alive. As he was beginning to take the roof from his shelter and scatter it back to the earth, he noticed an old man standing at the far end of his camp watching him intently. Grandfather was shocked that he hadn't been aware of the old man's arrival. Certainly he should have known of his approach miles before he got to camp. But there was something about the way that this old one blended perfectly into the jungle that told Grandfather he was not dealing with an ordinary person. As Grandfather gazed at the old one, the old man smiled warmly and waved. As Grandfather waved back, the old man vanished into the jungle without a trace, right before Grandfather's eyes.

Grandfather was startled at how easily the old one had slipped away. As he searched the immediate area with his eyes, he began to believe that this old man was in fact a spirit, not of flesh at all. That is the only way that he could have made it right into Grandfather's camp without being detected. Grandfather simply shrugged off the experience and went back to work, trying now to understand why this spirit had come to him. As he thought about the incident, he realized how the old one had been dressed. Though his lower body was clothed in a small loincloth, his headdress was made of beautiful bright green feathers, the likes of which he had never seen before. Everything else about the old one told of his native heritage. Possibly this man spirit was at one time a member of a tribe that once lived in the area.

As Grandfather continued working, deep in thought, he felt a hand touch his shoulder and he turned around with a start. The old man stood before him, as if appearing from nowhere. Grandfather was startled again that he did not hear his approach. The old one seemed to be invisible in the cadence and flow of the forest, blending perfectly with his surroundings. Still assuming that the old one was spirit, Grandfather slowly reached out and touched the old man's shoulder. The old man did the same to Grandfather and they both laughed. With that the old one waved to the bushes and several young men stood up. Grandfather was absolutely flabbergasted that so many people had gotten right into his camp without being noticed. He knew that his energy was low and his awareness shrouded in sickness, but to him this was impossible. He must have looked so startled that the group began to laugh, not at Grandfather, but with him.

The old one seemed to sense that Grandfather was in pain and sickened. He gently reached out and felt Grandfather's head, then retracted his hand and said something in a language that Grandfather could not understand. Grandfather trembled uncontrollably, but did not know why. The next thing Grandfather remembered was that the jungle began to spin and he collapsed to the ground. He could feel kind and gentle hands lifting him, but he could not piece together the events that followed. All he remembered was movement, passing jungle, and the feeling of being carried. His whole world seemed to spin uncontrollably. Thought became impossible and he seemed to be living in some surrealistic dream world. Then all was black. Time and place seemed no longer to exist.

Grandfather remembered waking up in a strange shelter, feeling very groggy. He tried to piece together the events that got him there but everything remained a blur of events. All he could clearly remember was the old man who had come to his camp. He was frightened at first but this passed as he looked around the shelter more closely and saw it was primitive. This gave him a certain sense of security that he was in good hands with these ancient people. He sensed that they were much like him, though he did not know why. He did know that he was beginning to feel better, much better than he had in many days, though he had no idea as to how he got there or how long he had been asleep. There was evidence all around him that people had come and gone through the entire ordeal. He felt at peace.

He heard a shuffling at the doorway and in walked the old man who he had seen in his camp. A big smile spread across the old man's face as he looked at Grandfather. They both tried to communicate in words, but to no avail. Realizing that words now were useless, the old man pointed to Grandfather's lower leg and lifted a leaf bandage from his calf. To Grandfather's amazement there was a badly swollen area, definitely caused by some sort of a bite, probably an insect of some sort. The old one made a gesture to his head, feigning fainting and fever, and Grandfather finally understood. Grandfather had vaguely remembered getting bitten by something several days earlier, but had paid it no attention. It was around the same time of the bite that Grandfather remembered growing very weak and losing his appetite. At the time he did not connect the two, but now he understood.

Grandfather finally realized that he had been poisoned by some insect and if it had not been for the old man, he probably would be dead by now. That was probably the reason that Grandfather had lost his awareness and inner vision and did not see the approach of the old man and the others. Throughout the day, Grandfather and the old man began to communicate as other people came in and out of the shelter bringing food and otherwise taking care of Grandfather. As time passed, Grandfather began to understand the old man a little better, though much of the communication was in a loose sign language. It did not take long before Grandfather knew that this old one was probably the herbalist or shaman of this little tribe, such was his ability and the other people's respect for him.

Grandfather was allowed to rest through the end of the day, without much more of a conversation. The old one sat by Grandfather throughout the evening and well into the night, rarely leaving his side for even a moment. Several times during the night Grandfather was awakened by the old one and given a strong tea to drink. Otherwise his sleep was peaceful and almost dreamless. When he awakened the next morning, he felt the best he had since he had left Mexico. The old man looked very pleased with Grandfather's progress, but would not allow him to sit up until he had something to eat. After drinking a strong tea and eating some delicious but unknown herbs and roots, Grandfather was helped into a sitting position. He could feel a nagging weakness deep inside, but he knew that it was on its way out.

Late in the morning the old man helped Grandfather to his feet. At first he was a bit shaky, but soon his strength returned. The bite on his leg was no longer swollen or painful but he could still see the deep punctures. The old one had intimated to Grandfather that he should have been dead from the bite long ago. The old one seemed amazed at how quickly Grandfather had healed. Grandfather and the old man began to sense something special about each other, something that bound them deeper than just the flesh. There was a mutual respect between them and they spent most of the morning and the remainder of the afternoon trying to communicate. The conversation was very slow and labored, but they began to understand each other on deeper levels than just words and sign language.

Grandfather was led around the small camp by the old man and introduced to various people. The old one pointed out the various shelters, the skills, and the way the people prepared the food. Most of the skills Grandfather had used before but what fascinated him the most were the plants that the people used both for food and for medication. For some reason Grandfather was interested in these with a passion. The old man, who Grandfather now knew as "Parrot," saw Grandfather's interest in the plants and began to concentrate his teaching efforts to that of the plants. Grandfather became a willing student, hanging on Parrot's every gesture. However, as the day wore on, Grandfather grew very tired again. Even the short journey around camp was a strain on him and he returned to the shelter to rest. It was at this time, when he laid down to sleep, that he was in the old man's bed, for the old one slept on the floor every night next to Grandfather.

For the next several days, Grandfather and Parrot stayed together. Parrot became a more than willing teacher and Grandfather an eager student. Parrot first showed Grandfather the various plants around the immediate camp area. They would collect the plants, prepare them, cook them, and finally eat them. This way, the spirit of the plant could be fully understood and remembered. So too did Grandfather learn how to make up and use the various medicinal plants of the jungle. He was intrigued at how similar the effects were as compared to the plants that he always worked with. With each passing day they went farther and farther out into the jungle, where more exotic plants could be found. The old man was treating Grandfather much like he would any herbal apprentice, though Grandfather learned much faster.

Eventually, Parrot began to see Grandfather's deeper spiritual side and realized that Grandfather must be a healer for his own tribe. It was at this point that Parrot began to treat Grandfather as his equal rather than just a student. It was not long before Grandfather began to teach Parrot of his ways. Grandfather also began to teach the various other tribal members about traps, tracking, and his methods of survival. Grandfather was eventually treated with as much respect from the people as was Parrot. The two became very close friends and Parrot even allowed Grandfather to help treat many of his patients. Sometimes Parrot would allow Grandfather to treat his patient alone. To them, it was delightful to be able to mix medicines and skills. Grandfather felt at home with his adopted people.

As the months slipped by, Grandfather and Parrot began to understand and communicate with each other a lot faster. It was not long before they both realized that even though their cultures were many thousands of miles apart, there were more things similar than different. In the practice of medicine and the wisdom of the spirit they were almost identical in philosophy and technique. Grandfather began to understand that a common thread bound his people to these people of the Amazon jungles. Eventually, neither Grandfather nor Parrot saw any differences. This realization helped Grandfather confirm that all the people of the earth shared a common truth, a common thread that bound them all together into one spiritual consciousness. He still had his doubts concerning the white man and his various religions however.

Grandfather stayed with these people for the better part of a year. Eventually he built his own shelter, participated in hunting and gathering parties, took an important part in their various ceremonies, and otherwise became a full working member of the little tribe. Most of all, he and Parrot attended to the many ills, both physical and spiritual, of the people. They formed a deep bond between them, a deeper friendship than either of them had yet known. They considered each other brothers in the truest sense of the word. Once, they took a journey together to one of the most sacred areas that Parrot had known. There they worshiped for several days together, entering into what Grandfather would consider a vision quest. It was during this time that the bittersweet realization that Grandfather would be leaving soon was understood.

Grandfather stayed with the little tribe for a few more weeks and then finally one day he was gone before the camp awoke. Parrot understood, like Grandfather, that this was the right way to part. Nothing left to be said, no good-byes, but just the deep sense of knowing that they would always be together. Still, there was a tremendous sadness and sense of loss that they would both suffer. Though no one knew exactly the day that Grandfather would be leaving, Grandfather found a beautiful long bow by his side when he awakened that morning. It belonged to Parrot and was the bow he used to learn this tribe's way of hunting. On the end of the limb were two long green feathers and one red feather. It was the symbol of the everlasting bond between Grandfather and Parrot, between Grandfather's people and the people of the jungle.

Grandfather wandered up the Amazon and deep into the jungle as he had planned to do more than a year ago. Now armed with his new knowledge of the local plants and the way of the jungle, his travels became easy. It was as effortless as living in his homeland and for the first time he really felt part of the jungle. As the days passed by and he reached deeper into the jungle, he understood why the people of the earth were closely bound together in spiritual consciousness. It was the earth that bound them and created the common thread. Here he felt at home, for all the earth now was his home. It was the earth that was the common philosophy and purity. The same bonds that tied Grandfather to Parrot and his people also bound them to the earth. It was common ground to all who walk the sacred path.

The spirit constantly compelled Grandfather to go deeper into the jungle. Grandfather instinctively knew that there was much more that he had to learn from the jungle, a knowledge that would tend to tie everything he had learned together. He never camped for more than a night in any one location. Instead he kept on moving, feeding as did the animals, foraging along the way, and rarely stopping to cook anything. For most of the journey he ate nothing but the plants. Only once did he supplement his vegetarian diet with a fish. The jungle seemed to dictate to him that he needed only the plants on this type of journey and his health and energy remained high. He was learning to listen to the jungle as it taught him the plants, and sensitized his inner vision to that of the jungle consciousness.

Finally, Grandfather felt that he could not go any deeper into the jungle. It was not because he was physically unable to, but spiritually he felt that this was where he was supposed to be. It did not take Grandfather long before he found a beautiful camp area, not far from a little waterfall. He could feel that the waterfall was important, for it had an undeniable spiritual presence that beckoned him to it. It was a special place, a sacred place of power, and he wondered if Parrot knew of this place. Within the span of two days, Grandfather's camp was built and his food stores filled. He then concentrated on spiritual things, visiting the waterfall religiously, to pray and listen to the voice of the jungle. Without fail, every sunrise and sunset was met at the waterfall. Sometimes Grandfather would spend the entire day in and around the falls.

One afternoon Grandfather looked up from the water and was startled to see a very old man standing on the bank, looking at him. He had appeared much the same way that Parrot had and at first Grandfather thought that it might be Parrot. But this man was too old to be Parrot, yet the mannerisms were much the same. The old man waved to Grandfather and Grandfather returned the gesture with a broad smile. Grandfather realized that the waterfall had blotted out all outside sound, but he should have noted the approach of the old man long before he appeared on the bank. Grandfather instantly knew that this old man must be a shaman, for his appearance and attitude were of that consciousness. So too did Parrot move about the jungle in this way and Grandfather felt an instant bond between himself and the old man. There was something very familiar about him.

The old man motioned to Grandfather to follow him and Grandfather went without hesitation. The old one moved quickly through the jungle, disturbing nothing as he passed. The old man disappeared far up ahead and it wasn't long before Grandfather entered a small clearing. At one end of the clearing was a small and simple hut, much the same as Parrot's shelter, only smaller and more primitive. Grandfather saw that the old one had gone inside, and he followed. As Grandfather entered the shelter he was startled to see not only the old man but also sitting near him was Parrot. The resemblance between the two was striking. Grandfather understood immediately that Parrot and this old man were somehow related. Possibly, Grandfather thought, the old man was in fact Parrot's teacher and guide.

Parrot introduced Grandfather to the old man and Grandfather's suspicions were confirmed. This old man was not only Parrot's teacher but also his blood grandfather. Parrot told Grandfather that the old man's name translated out to mean "he-who-has-no-name." The reason for this, Parrot told Grandfather, was because No Name had transcended the tribe, the religion, and even his identity. He was truly a child of the earth, and lived without the need of many of the spiritual toys and crutches that still bind men to the flesh. No Name had been the teacher of many shamans but now preferred to live alone, close to the jungle consciousness. Parrot told Grandfather that the shamans came to this place, to this small but sacred waterfall, for spiritual renewal and to learn the wisdom of No Name.

Grandfather was more than delighted to see Parrot again. They hugged each other for a long time and cried. Grandfather always knew that he would see Parrot again but not so soon. Yet somehow he suspected that he would see him here near the waterfall. Grandfather was even more captivated with No Name. This old one reminded Grandfather of his own great-grandfather. No Name seemed to have the same unspoken wisdom that Grandfather had seen in Coyote Thunder. Within a few hours a great bond was formed between the three men. Grandfather and Parrot became No Name's students for many weeks to come, and Grandfather began to look upon No Name the same way he looked upon his own great-grandfather. This old one possessed the jungle wisdom that he desperately wanted to know. He knew that the spirit had led him to this place to meet and learn from No Name, and now there was no doubt in his mind.

The three did not concentrate on the physical identification of plants, or for that matter anything else tangible to the flesh. Instead, they discussed philosophy and learned No Name's approach to the many things of the spirit. Grandfather here again saw a similarity and correlation to what he understood and believed. It was confirmed that there could be no separation between the people of the earth. They were of one mind and heart. The fabric of spiritual consciousness ran through them all. So too did Grandfather realize that when one truly walks the shamanic path he transcends all religions, doctrine, ceremonies, and even the people. Here on this path all shamans, no matter where they are from or how they learned the wisdom of the spirit, walk as one and have one mind. How they arrived on this path no longer makes a difference and they speak a common knowledge and tongue.

Grandfather held No Name in awe. This old man had truly found the final path to spiritual enlightenment. In that path, Grandfather found a certain and pure simplicity, unencumbered by any of man's complications. It was this simplicity that Grandfather had sought for so long. It was this simplicity that Grandfather wanted to live. The old one was living proof that the quest of the spirit was not difficult but free and pure. It was man and his quest to define and complicate the wisdom of the spirit that made the path difficult. Grandfather knew that he too had transcended most religious crutches and now No Name showed him the way to abandon the rest. On one particular morning, the camp was deftly abandoned. Grandfather wandered back to the north, Parrot returned to his people, and No Name vanished into the vast expanse of the jungle. Parting was painful and loneliness had already begun to set in, but there was sweet joy of the sharing and communication that bonded the two men together, forever.

As I sat at the campfire that night listening to Grandfather's story and holding the old bow, I could feel how sacred the bow was. To Grandfather it was not just the skill of hunting, but the embodiment of all that he had learned on his first trip into the deep jungles. I was amazed to tears to hear Grandfather talk of a common path and how all shamans spoke a common tongue. Most of all I was intrigued by the simplicity and interconnectedness of it all. From that point on the old bow became a symbol of simplicity to me also. I finally understood what Grandfather had meant when he spoke of a "oneness." It was not just the oneness of flesh and spirit, but also the oneness with all things, all philosophies.

8

The Priest

It was not long after Grandfather had told Rick and I of his first journey to South America that I began to get deeply bothered by something Grandfather had said during the story. He had said that all of the people of the earth were connected on a spiritual level. It was these children of the earth that shared a common belief, a common ground. Though their beliefs were slightly different in approach, they were almost identical in the final analysis. However, Grandfather could not say the same of the white man's religions, and that was the reason for my deep pondering. I did not know whether Grandfather had meant that he thought that the white man's religions were fraudulent, or if he just did not know. After all, for a while I was raised in the white man's religion and I could not believe that it was wrong. The sheer thought of it bothered me for days and I began to brood about it frequently.

One night while sitting around the campfire, Grandfather asked me if there was something in the story of his journey to South American that had bothered me. He told me that he noticed that my mood had changed soon after he

121

had told the story and now he wanted to know why. I did not want to hurt Grandfather's feelings, nor did I want my worst fears to be confirmed, so I was a little hesitant in answering Grandfather's question. Instead I tended to circumvent the question and ask about other unrelated parts of Grandfather's journey. It did not take Grandfather long to realize what was bothering me. Instead of asking me about that which still remained unspoken, he immediately began to tell me the story of a priest, which I knew would ultimately answer my unasked question.

Grandfather had been slowly wandering back from his first trip to South America when he encountered the priest. He had not been driven in his travels since he left the jungle and rather took his time throughout the entire journey. He wanted to stay in areas longer so that he could explore the various landscapes and try to find teachers along the way. The spirit that usually drove him on his journeys and quests had remained silent for many months. He was very content just to learn as much as he could. Many times he stopped along the way for several weeks, especially in the places of old Mayan and Incan ruins. He knew that these places were spiritually active and he wanted to know all there was to know. Though he was not familiar with these cultures, he sensed something similar to his own philosophy.

He would search out anyone who still practiced the old religion, but many times he could not find a teacher. Some of the old ones that he encountered told him that their original religion had changed and changed again, and became more complicated every time. Still, there was the simplicity that No Name had so often spoken of that could be found in the complication. Grandfather knew through the story shared by these old people that these cultures had been destroyed much as had the culture of the tribes of the United States. Here too greed and the consciousness of destruction had almost entirely removed a people and their religion from the face of the earth. Grandfather could not understand how the white man's religions could permit him to create the destruction without fear of punishment or reprimand from that which the white man called God.

One late afternoon, seated high up in an old Mayan temple that overlooked the jungle, Grandfather was compelled again by the spirit. He had been looking toward the north, thinking deeply about the question of white man's religion when he knew that he had to leave this place and journey north. There was no doubt in his mind now that his many months of rest and leisure would soon come to an end. Even as he walked down the steps of the temple, he knew that he could not wait for the morning to leave but had to go immediately. To remain for even a few more hours would only produce a deep restlessness that would prevent any kind of rest, sleep, or even preparation for the journey. There was no hesitation or afterthought, for Grandfather just walked to his camp, scattered it to the earth, and headed north under the night sky.

As is typical for this type of journey, or quest, he did not camp for more than a night in any place. Just enough time was spent to replenish supplies and then it was back to the trail again. As he reached the deserts of Mexico, more time had to be spent gathering water, and that slowed his progress as usual. This time, the spirit did not lead him up the West Coast but straight through the center and into the hottest and most barren deserts. However, these conditions Grandfather knew very well and the travel was easy. Most people would perish under the same conditions, but Grandfather flourished. The earth took good care of him and he obeyed its every law. The farther north he traveled the more the spiritual voice inside nagged at him.

For the last few days of his travel, the spirit would not allow him to stop, rest, eat, or even sleep. Grandfather could sense an urgency in the spiritual drive and he had to obey it without question. He began to push himself to the limits of his endurance. The lack of sleep caused Grandfather to hallucinate at times and made travel very difficult. Several times he nearly fell to sleep standing up. Since he could not stop, his water supply began to dwindle and he had to ration the rest severely, which only added to his pain. Finally, late in the last night of the journey, he came upon a high ridge where he knew that he had to make camp and get some rest. Though the area he had been led to would not be an ideal location, he sensed that this was where the spirit wanted him to be. He built a meager shelter between some huge boulders and quickly fell into a long and unconscious sleep.

He was abruptly awakened the next day by the sound of a bell ringing in the distance. It took Grandfather quite a while to regain a sense of time, place, and reality, such was the intensity of his profound sleep. After regaining consciousness and realizing that the sound of the bell was a reality and not a dream, he cautiously crawled from his boulder shelter. Carefully he climbed to the top of the ridge, staying very low to the rocky ground. It was apparent now that there must be some kind of settlement below that he had overlooked in his fatigue of the night before. From the ringing of the bell he knew that it must be that of the white man. As he peered over the side, he was startled to see a small adobe church, surrounded by other adobe structures, all in poor repair.

Grandfather suspiciously eyed the little hamlet. Except for the ringing of the bell, the compound looked utterly deserted. There was no sign of human or animal. The few wagons that were around were badly broken and deteriorated by the harsh desert weather. Grandfather knew however that there must be someone there as the bell was ringing and there were still a few human tracks around the front of the church. He watched the compound and buildings for the better part of the morning, long after the bell had stopped ringing. Finally a few people emerged from the church. They were poorly dressed and looked to be near the edge of starvation. Their journey back to their houses looked labored and painful, showing clearly the way the desert was beating them. Finally, from the huge door of the small church stepped a very old priest, or "black robe" as Grandfather called them. He looked as badly worn as did the rest of the people.

Grandfather watched him cross the courtyard and head slowly in the direction of the ridge where Grandfather was watching. As the priest drew close to the outer edge of the compound, Grandfather could plainly see that the "black robe" was not like other black robes he encountered before. The robe was tattered, torn, and a dry soil color. The old priest did not look very healthy at all. There too was a pain and weariness in his walk. Grandfather had to shift his position closer to the edge of the cliff to follow the priest. The priest continued to the bottom of the cliff and to the remnants of a small well. The priest then lowered a bucket into the well, but did not seem to retrieve any water. It was obvious then to Grandfather why these people looked so badly; they were out of water. Grandfather watched the old priest kneel by the side of the well, apparently in prayer.

Grandfather felt a powerful calling to go down to the priest. The driving force was so strong that he had to set aside his fears and obey. He still feared the white man, and this priest was definitely a white man, though no one in the compound looked strong enough to do Grandfather any harm. However, he knew the power of white man's guns. It doesn't take a strong man to be a warrior with a gun, so his climb down the cliff was slow, cautious, and very quiet. He did not want the priest to see him until he could determine if the Priest was a threat or not. Grandfather moved like a shadow, deftly shifting his position to a point where he could get a clear view of the priest without being seen. As usual, with Grandfather's skill of a scout, this became a very simple process.

Grandfather was close enough to hear the priest's every word, and was startled by what he was saying. The priest spoke in Spanish, a language that Grandfather could barely understand, but the meaning came through. The priest prayed, "Holy Earth Mother, the physical manifestation of God's love, help us. My people are without water, our wells have run dry, and we are dying. Many have lost faith and have run away to other places, but those who remain still believe that we must be here. Oh, God, we need your help." Grandfather immediately knew that this old priest had to know something of the Native people and what they believed, such was the wisdom and intensity of his prayers. To Grandfather's astonishment the priest called out and said to Grandfather, "Come here, brother." Grandfather could not believe that anyone could have detected his presence there, but he stood and moved toward the old priest, without question.

Grandfather moved to the other side of the old well, using the old rock wall as the last buffer between himself and the old priest. In the old priest's face, Grandfather detected a kindness, the reasons for which could not be put into words. Grandfather began to reluctantly move toward the old priest as he beckoned Grandfather to him. Grandfather detected no sense of threat from the old priest, but rather an unconditional acceptance. As Grandfather moved closer to the priest, the priest said, "You must have been sent by

God. You are one of the children of this land. Would you please show this old priest in what way to ask our Earth Mother how to get water from this old well?" Grandfather was struck speechless by what the old priest was saying. From everything he had heard about the "black robes" this statement was totally out of character.

Grandfather sat down by the old priest and listened to what he had to say. First the priest introduced himself as Father Juan and then went on to tell Grandfather of his plight. He had lived here for many years, with a small community of people who just barely eeked a living from this barren land. Several years earlier, the well began to run dry during various times of the year. Now in the past year it had been without water more times than not. Because of the water shortage, many of his people had left the area and had gone off to find better places to live. The old priest wanted to leave long ago, but he felt that God wanted him to stay here and he had to obey. He told Grandfather that every day he came to the well to pray for water, but to no avail.

To Grandfather, Father Juan seemed like a very sincere and dedicated man. Even though the water had not returned to the well, the old priest would not lose faith. Without hesitation, Grandfather told the priest that he could help him find some water for his people. In Grandfather's heart he knew that there was still water around, but no longer in the place of the existing well. The vegetation, the color of the earth, and the faint smell of water in the air confirmed Grandfather's decision. Grandfather then climbed down into the deep well as Father Juan looked on. He felt and smelled the walls of the well, and dug a little in the earth at the deepest place. Though the sands were dry to the touch, they were not dusty. Grandfather suspected that the well still contained water but at a deeper level than the well had been dug.

Climbing out of the well, Grandfather explained to Father Juan that the well was not deep enough. He told the priest that was the reason that the well ran dry periodically through the year. It was only during the wet seasons that the well would produce if left in this way. It had also been very dry, almost a drought, for the past several years and that is why the well would no longer produce. As Grandfather talked, he could see tears forming in the old priest's eyes, and a look of thanksgiving on his face. Instantly, Grandfather could sense something different about this old man. To Grandfather he seemed more like Coyote Thunder or No Name than he did a priest. There was the same air about him, the same feeling of "oneness" that Grandfather could feel in other shamans. He could not explain the feeling, for it conflicted with all that he had heard about the white man's religion.

The priest called out toward the village and two men came running toward them carrying buckets and shovels. They looked at the priest and then at Grandfather skeptically, yet they obeyed Father Juan when he asked them to help Grandfather dig the well. Grandfather climbed into the well despite the priest's comments that he had done enough. Grandfather dug for most of the morning without stopping and by high sun, he had hit water. As the bucket of soil mixed with water was hoisted to the surface, Grandfather could hear the cheering. With each subsequent bucket he heard more and more voices cheering and talking, though he could not tell how many. Within the next hour, the well was above Grandfather's chest with water and he could dig no more. As he slowly climbed back up the side, buckets on tethers began to come over the side hoisting the water past him.

As he emerged from the top side of the well, he was met with a small cheering crowd. As he stepped away from the well, Father Juan walked right up to him and gave him a big affectionate hug. Clearly, Grandfather saw that the priest was crying. Father Juan then turned to the small crowd and exclaimed, "This is truly a miracle. This man has been sent by God to bring us back our water. This man knows the voice of our Earth Mother and the earth told him where she had water." Grandfather was shocked at the priest's statement. He did not feel like he had been sent by anyone, for it seemed just by chance that he had arrived here when he did. He told the priest so, but Father Juan responded, saying, "Then what is it that drove you so far out of your path? What power was it that guided you here?"

There was no question in Grandfather's mind that the priest was right. He had been driven to this place, especially near the end of his journey. It was the spirit within him that had led him here at just the right time to help these people. There was no denying that the priest could see much deeper than Grandfather had originally given him credit for. Grandfather, at this point, began to see that the priest knew much more than he was letting on to his congregation, or to Grandfather. Yet as they looked at each other, they could both sense the power in the other. There was a mutual respect, a common ground that they both seemed to share. As the people hoisted bucket after bucket of water from the well, Father Juan asked Grandfather if he would stay with the people for a while, and teach them of the earth.

Grandfather was a bit hesitant at first, but he knew in his heart that was why he was led to this place. He also knew it was not just that he had to find water for the people, for it seemed like there was much more to learn before he moved on. He now could finally understand the urgency of why the spirit had driven him so hard these past few days. He could plainly see that these people had no water at all and probably would have been dead within the next several days. He could also feel a deep draw toward the old priest. This old one was someone special, much like No Name, and he sensed that this was who the spirit had guided him to see. It took the well and the problem of the water to bring them together. Grandfather did not believe in coincidence, and knew that he had been sent.

Grandfather decided to take things one day at a time. He had no sense of how long he was to stay in this place. At first he would not enter the church. Fear from all the stories that he had heard about conversion and brainwashing still haunted him. He would not even sleep near the compound at night but chose to go back up on the ridge. He did not like the feeling of confinement that he felt in the compound and preferred the freedom of his camp. Each morning at sunrise, then again at sunset, Grandfather would sit and pray. He was startled to see that the old priest did the same as he. The old priest seemed to have a special spot on the land, as did Grandfather. Several times, they waved to each other as they went to their areas. It then struck Grandfather that if the priest could pray in his church, that of the temples of creation, then he could go and pray in the priest's church. From that point on, Grandfather had no apprehension about entering the church.

With each passing day, Grandfather began to respect and admire this old priest. They would sit up in the hills for hours teaching each other and discussing religion, beliefs, and philosophy. Grandfather began to see a deeper connection between No Name and Father Juan. This old priest, though still believing in his religion, had expanded it beyond what his church taught. Father Juan, whether by accident or design, had indeed transcended his religion and now walked the shamanic path. Grandfather was startled to find that Father Juan believed in many of the things that Grandfather did. So too could Grandfather sense that the priest was trying to change some of the ways of the church, and that was probably why he ended up in this place.

It was not long before Grandfather and Father Juan began to pray together each night on the ridge. They would discuss the wisdom of the spirit well into the night, and soon Grandfather found how deep Father Juan's philosophy ran. Grandfather soon discovered that Father Juan's path was almost identical to Grandfather's, though he approached it in a different way. The end results were the same. Father Juan told Grandfather of his endless years of spiritual searching, asceticism, and working with the people of the earth. He told Grandfather that at first he wanted to convert the Native Americans, but as he grew older, he began to listen to what they had to say. The first thing that the old priest learned was that they all prayed to the same God. This became evident whenever the priest prayed, for he always began the prayer with "God, Great Spirit, You who are called by so many names, and worshiped in so many ways . . ."

Father Juan also told Grandfather that he believed that the earth was the physical manifestation of the Creator's love, and we should take care of His gifts. He also said that to him the earth did feel like a mother and all the things of the earth were his brothers and sisters. Father Juan told Grandfather of the man called St. Francis, who could actually walk with the wild animals and knew them as friends. The old priest seemed as interested in Grandfather's philosophy as Grandfather was in his. They began to compare. When Grandfather would tell Father Juan something he believed, Father Juan would find evidence of it in his religion. When Father Juan quoted the Bible, Grandfather would show the priest evidence in Grandfather's beliefs. It was obvious to them both that they were finding a common truth, the life blood of theirs and of all beliefs.

Grandfather spent the season with the old priest. He showed the priest's now growing congregation how to work the fields more effectively. He taught them how to care for the earth to work in balance with its power. He also taught them to listen to the many voices of the earth, and have faith that the Creator would provide. Most of all, Grandfather and the priest spent every available hour together. They taught each other, creating even a broader understanding than either could ever imagine. In the end, Grandfather began to look at the priest with the same sense of brotherhood as he had No Name and Parrot. There was no doubt in Grandfather's mind that the white man's religion was part of all philosophies, and through that belief, anyone could learn to walk the path of the shaman.

Most of all, what Grandfather learned from the priest was the wisdom of Christ. Grandfather could not understand, however, how the simple teachings of Christ had become so complicated. Christ had no church, for he taught in the mountains, in the gardens, and in the wilderness, and his teaching was simple truth. When Grandfather confronted Father Juan with this question, Father Juan told him that was why he was a priest. Father Juan felt that his mission in life, similar to Grandfather's, was to find and reestablish the simple truth, free of man's meddling and complications, then pass this truth on to others despite what anyone thought.

In the final days together, Grandfather taught the priest how to use the sweat lodge and why it was a universal spiritual truth for all who used it. Their first and last sweat together was a richly spiritual experience. Two men from different cultures, different ages, and different beliefs, both praying to the same God. As Grandfather headed back to his people he felt another great sense of loss and like the connection to Parrot and No Name, Grandfather could feel the same connection between Father Juan and himself. Grandfather knew in his heart that someday the philosophy of Father Juan would spread across the land. He also knew that he would never see Father Juan again in the flesh, but knew that they would pray together again in their shared world of spirit.

My mind was at peace after I heard the story of Grandfather and Father Juan. I could see now that Grandfather felt that all religions and beliefs were connected by the same spirit. Grandfather knew that all paths finally led to the Great Spirit providing man can reach the purity of his religion and see past all the religious dogmas. I also, at this point, vowed to be as open as Grandfather had been to all philosophies and religions. I finally understood that they all had something to teach. There was no right or wrong, just the truth.

From Grandfather's story of the priest, I've learned to be open to all people, no matter what their religions or beliefs. I have learned to forget that I have a past and empty my cup so that I could listen to people purely, without their teachings being filtered through my own prejudice. I've learned to listen and then to work my way through their words and arrive at the common truth. Through this I have learned that there are more things common to all the various religions and beliefs of the world than there are in conflict. Once I realized this common truth I have been able to accept that there is but one truth, just many different paths leading there.

9

The Waterfall

Rick, Grandfather, and I had been heading back to camp on a trail that we called Drudgery. We began our journey long before sunrise and had walked through the better part of the day. It was mid-August, the temperatures were well into the nineties, the air was still and heavy with humidity. The entire dusty route was without water, and since we carried none, by mid-afternoon our throats were parched and our lips were cracked. The sun burned down, torturing and drying our flesh, and the dust rose in columns behind us, choking us with each step. All Rick and I could think about and talk about was getting to water. Eventually we could not even talk anymore such was the dryness of our throats.

As I dragged along I could almost envision the stream that ran through our camp. That would be the first water we would come to in over fourteen hours and it would be a soothing relief. I imagined what it would be like to plunge in, swimming and drinking at the same time, as I had done so many times before. My pace became a crawl as I dragged my feet and intensified the dust plumes. I also began to trip frequently and a few times actually stumbled to the ground.

133

Each time it became harder to get back up and face the trail again. It was not so much the fatigue that I felt due to the deep sands, but the intense thirst that made the trip so difficult. Several times I hallucinated water. Sometimes I could feel it in the air, other times I could faintly hear it running, and once I thought I could actually see the water far up ahead. Consciously I knew that there was no water along this trail and it became a struggle between reality and hallucination each time the sense of water filtered into my mind.

I could tell that Rick was as bad off as I was. Neither of us looked around or smiled. There was no conversation and each of us seemed wrapped up in our own little trusty vacuum of dust. Not so with Grandfather. He would pause frequently to study a track, a flower, or a feeding bird. The smile never left his face and he seemed to enjoy every moment, apparently free of thirst. It became exasperating to us every time he stopped for we too had to stop, which would only prolong our agony and eventual arrival at the water. Grandfather's pace was not even slowed in the least and with each passing mile he seemed to gain more energy rather than lose it as we were doing. I imagined that he was somehow being sustained by the very landscape itself, thriving on that which only brought us thirst. In a way, his attitude and buoyancy made me feel a bit angry. Not at him but at myself.

As we drew closer to our camp area and the eventual soothing and quenching properties of the stream, our pace quickened. Though we still dragged our feet and stumbled, our focus on the stream seemed to carry us along. As we entered the camp trail our stumbled walk shifted into a brisk walk, then a run, and finally a sprint. It became a race against thirst, as if we could outrun it and lose it in the water. We ran right through camp without even a break in stride, down the stream trail, and finally plunging lustily into the cool and refreshing waters. Even as I dove beneath the surface I began to drink, holding my breath as long as I could as I gobbled down huge mouthfuls. Rick and I then lay back in the water imagining our bodies hissing like the sound that water makes when it hits the hot rocks in a sweat lodge. It did not take long for the thirst to become a distant memory as our strength and energy began to return.

Rick and I lay back at the edge of the stream, our heads resting on the shore and our bodies still submerged in the water. As I lay there, I watched Grandfather walking leisurely down the trail, stopping every so often to study some unknown mystery. He was not at all in a hurry, but rather took his time. To someone who did not know any better they would have never known that he had just finished the same long trek that we had. He seemed so totally unaffected by the whole trip, the intense thirst, or the need to get to the water as we had been. To him, it appeared, it was just another stroll, a leisurely walk, where neither water nor heat was a factor at all. He just looked so serene and unhurried that he made me angry at myself again. I imagined all of the wondrous things that I had overlooked because of the intense thirst that had clouded my consciousness and perception.

Grandfather approached the stream as he always did, smiling at me and Rick, then finally turning his full attention to the water. He paused for a long time and gazed into its depths. His attitude was one of prayer, of thanksgiving, and of rapture. At no time did he seem in a hurry to drink; instead he took his time, where every action seemed to be so slow and deliberate. Finally, he stooped and touched the water, eventually stroking its surface, all the while in passionate prayer. It was a long time before his hands finally cupped the water and he drank, savoring each mouthful much like a wine taster savors a vintage wine.

This action never ceased to amaze Rick and me, even though Grandfather went through it every time he approached water to drink. It made little difference to Grandfather the intensity of his thirst, for there was always the prayer of thanksgiving and the impassioned touching of the waters, yet the ritual always seemed to be prolonged during the times of extreme thirst. Anyone who saw him would immediately see and feel the intensity of Grandfather's sense of thanksgiving and awe. So too would anyone who bore witness to this act be held in awe. Rick and I just turned to each other and smiled in a knowing way. A kind of knowing without fully knowing, for we could only vaguely understand the driving force that directed Grandfather's actions.

Rick and I spent much of the day and early evening in and around the water. Water for me always is a source of tranquillity, a meditation, where I can think more clearly and deeply. It always tends to cleanse the body and spirit, intensifying spiritual thoughts. This day was no exception. I thought about many things but most of all I thought about Grandfather's approach to the water. Even though he had given me numerous explanations on numerous occasions, I still felt that he was holding something back. There always seemed to be a piece of the puzzle missing and without that missing piece I could not fully understand his actions and deep sense of thanksgiving. I could sense in a way that it went far beyond the parameters of thanksgiving, and it was what lay beyond that I fully wanted to understand. I became determined to find the answer as soon as the opportunity arose.

After dark, Grandfather, Rick, and I sat around the campfire and talked about our long journey. Both Rick and I talked of the intense thirst and how it had obliterated all else. We also told Grandfather how disappointed we were that we gave in to the negative effects of the thirst and how we wished that we were more like him. He simply told us that we had given the thirst far too much power over us and it was this power that cut us off from the beauties found all along our walk. Without hesitation I asked Grandfather if he was not also thirsty and why he always took his time, even in times of dire thirst, before he would drink water.

Grandfather then told me again that it was in reverence and thanksgiving that he approached the water in this way, just as he had always explained it to me. But this time I told him I thought there had to be much more to it than that. I felt there was something that he was leaving out, whether by accident or on purpose, and I wanted to know why. He looked at Rick and me for a long time, then finally told us the story of the waterfall, which forever changed his perception of life.

It was during Grandfather's last trip to South America that he was taught one of the most profound lessons of his life by this waterfall. He was visiting an old shaman that he had visited many times before when he was told of the waterfall, which this old man called, simply, "life." Grandfather was told that the waterfall was deep in the jungle and that the journey to its base would take several days. The old shaman told Grandfather that the waterfall must be approached alone, thus he could only point the direction and not lead him there. He told Grandfather that only those who walked a spiritual path could find this waterfall; all others would perish on the perilous journey through the jungle.

Grandfather began his journey to the waterfall on the following morning, using the shaman's directions and his own inner vision to guide him. The jungle was thick and trackless at this point, for the old shaman lived alone, far from the village, and his shelter was located on the outermost part of the encampment. There were no trails beyond his shelter and the trees were so thick and the underbrush so overgrown that he could hardly see the sun at all. There were no natural features to give him a sense of direction and he found that he had to rely solely on his inner vision to guide him. At times he found that even in the middle of the day, much of his journey was in deep green darkness. It was a tough journey, for Grandfather did not want to kill any plants or break them out of his way. Thus he crawled under or walked around the thicker stands of vegetation, which only made his journey longer and completely obscured his sense of direction.

The nights were even worse than the days. His determination to find the waterfall of life was so strong that many times he would travel through the night, resting only when he could not physically go on. He felt that the journey had to be undertaken with this kind of drive so as to show the spirits and the waterfall that he was truly worthy to be on such a quest. So too at times did he know that he was truly lost. Not only was he unsure as to where he was, but he could not get back to the old shaman without the use of his inner vision. His inner vision was all that he had and he had to trust it fully, casting out all logical doubt and giving himself over completely to his spiritual mind.

The journey took many days, but he did not remember how many. He said that the days and nights were fused together in a random sort of way where it made little difference to him if it were day or night, or even how long the journey would take. All he knew was that he had to get to the waterfall, or die trying. He had no fear, for he knew that the jungle, like any other wilderness, was still part of the earth and that it would take care of him. To him it was home; for that matter, any wild place was his home. Though he wanted desperately to get to the waterfall, he took the time to study and communicate with the various plants and animals along the way. There was no rush, never a rush.

He studied the landscape; searching out its secrets, he found no evidence of human travel. Most of the trails were made from small animals, which would not allow for easy human travel. Even when he dug beneath the layers of loam, there was no sign of human footprints even in the more open areas. Grandfather had shown us, long ago, how to carefully dig through the forest litter and reveal tracks that had been hidden from the deteriorating effects of weather, some of which could be dated back many years. So, when Grandfather told us that he had no evidence of human travel, we could be assured that no one had passed through that part of the jungle. He sensed that he was one of the only humans to walk through this area. He imagined then what it felt like for the first man to ever walk upon the earth.

Grandfather remembered that for the last two days and nights of his journey, the landscape began to change. It was no longer flat jungle, and now he continuously began to climb higher and higher as he approached some unseen mountain range. The jungle was still too thick to see any distant change, but he could feel the elevation changes with each passing mile. Soon, large moss and fern-covered boulders began to appear in the jungle, small at first, but growing larger as he climbed higher and higher. Even the vegetation began to change as new plants and animals began to appear and the familiar ones began to grow uncommon.

As he traveled he sensed a deeper change than just the elevation and the jungle. There was something more, a power that he could not describe, but a power that seemed to beckon him, directing his every move. At first he could not place its origin. Even his inner vision failed him and this sense of unknowing followed him through much of the last day and night. It was nearing dawn of his final day of travel when he realized that it was the powerful presence of the waterfall that was calling him. It was nothing he heard or saw that brought him to this realization, just a sense of knowing that the waterfall called "life" was luring him.

As he traveled, now pulled by the power of the waterfall, his trek became easier. It was almost as if he were being guided solely by his spiritual mind, where his body fell away and became nonexistent. The farther he traveled, the easier became the route. At times he felt as if he were floating rather than walking, to a point where there was no longer any fatigue. The closer he got, the clearer and more expansive his mind became, to a point where he could actually see the waterfall in his mind and feel it moving within his body.

The power and sound of the waterfall could now be felt on a physical level, even though he was still quite some distance away. This power and sound began as a low vibration and gradually intensified as he drew nearer to the falls. He still could not see the waterfall for the jungle remained thick, and it was impossible to see more than a few yards ahead. At times the sound, vibration, and power grew so intense that he felt like the waterfall was all around him. At those times he had to stop and reorient himself to the call of the waters. The jungle seemed damper at this point and the vegetation lusher and healthier than it had been on the beginning of the trip.

As the sound of the waterfall intensified, so too did the lushness of the vegetation. It seemed to him that the plants were feeding on the falls' energy, growing healthier and stronger with their close proximity to the energy of the waterfall. Still there was no visual sighting, just the ever increasing sound and intensity of the falling water. With each step closer to the waterfall the vibration, energy, and power increased, almost thundering at times. The very earth, rocks, and trees seemed to tremble as he touched them and soon even the leaves of plants seemed to quiver. At times the quivering earth and thunderous sound was frightening, yet at the same time energizing and soothing.

Finally, Grandfather reached the stream and began following it upward. The stream was quite deep, yet slow moving and wide, quite unexpected since the waterfall still sounded powerful and he had suspected that the stream would run wild and thunderous. As he moved up along the stream he noticed that he was entering a deep gorge, yet he could not see very far up ahead, such was the thickness of the trees and low vegetation. As he moved deep into the gorge, he noticed that the trees were healthier and larger than anything he had yet encountered. Here the very earth vibrated with a thunderous sound, trembling almost as if it were made of flesh. His pulse quickened as he moved forward, anticipating that at any moment the falls would come into view.

Finally, as he rounded the last bend in the stream, the waterfall came into full view. He was so awestruck by its magnificence that he almost lost his balance and fell into the stream. The waterfall poured down the mountain of green, slicing into the jungle like a silver ribbon. From the upper part of the mountain, at least as far as his eye could see, the stream danced across boulders in a wild frenzy. It collected in a deep pool midway up the mountain, then poured over the lip in a straight drop. It was wide at the top to the midway point, but then funneled through a thick rock outcropping, exploding to a thunderous mass of spray that rained down into the basal pool. Here the waters boiled, then stilled as they continued down the lower stream.

He had seen larger and grander falls in his life, but there was something about this one that captivated his spirit. Right away he felt a deep kinship with the falls, as if it had been speaking to him all along. What's more was that it was just as he had envisioned it to be when the old shaman spoke of its existence. So too did he realize that this falls was very sacred and he stood trembling, like the earth and trees, in this temple of water. As soon as he saw the falls he felt pure and free of all thought, and his body and spirit felt cleansed and awake. He shook with anticipation, as if waiting for the falls to reveal its wisdom.

After he composed himself he searched for a place to sit and wait for the waterfall to speak. The trembling never left him, such was the power of the waterfall and his anticipation. As he moved closer to the base of the falls, the rockscape became slippery and treacherous. Each step had to be planned before he even attempted to move. It took him hours to move even a short distance and by the time he reached the base of the falls it was late afternoon. He found a boulder that rose above the boiling spray of the waterfall and here he decided to sit. It was like an island, sticking out of the mist, and the upper part was dry. It would afford a good view of the entire falls. To him it was as if he were seated on an altar.

It was not his intention to undertake a vision quest, for there was no questing needed. Instead he sat and waited for the waterfall to speak to him, much like a child waits for an elder to speak. He believed that the actual questing took place on the long journey to the falls, and now all he had to do was to humbly wait. At this point he did not care if the waterfall communicated to him at all. He felt blessed just by being in its powerful presence. To him, just being there was enough, and from being there he felt fulfilled and pure. Those were gifts enough.

Grandfather sat at the base of the waterfall all night, never leaving the boulder altar. He could not sleep, but drifted in and out of a dreamlike stupor. Many times his mind would wander back in time, paradoxically to those times in his life when he was in the desert. Several times he relived the times of his life when he almost died of thirst, and at the point of pain the thundering of the waterfall would yank him back to reality. He did not know why he thought so often of his thirsty memories, but they came freely and without warning. He imagined that somehow the waterfall was causing the memories to surface, but he did not know why. Any other thoughts seemed random and out of place, which soon returned to thoughts of the arid places and extreme thirst.

Dawn was a gorgeous mix of light and shadow that made the waterfall appear as a solid column of water rather than thundering spray. The falls seemed at this point to stand out in bold relief from the darkened rock face, appearing even more so as a living entity. In a way, this now living falls shocked him. Certainly he knew that water had a spirit all of its own, but this falls was more than spirit, it was now flesh to him. As he gazed at the falls there was no doubt in his mind that it was alive, not only alive, but had a mind of its own. It was a collective consciousness of every drop and fragment of spray, coming together to form the living mind of the waterfall. It was no longer the blood of Earth Mother, but now a living, thinking being.

He trembled at the thought of being in the presence of such a deity. To him it was a sudden enlightenment to realize that the water was not just spirit, but a living entity. He reveled in the thought. The waterfall had taught him what was to be the first of many lessons. Truly, Grandfather said that he thought, this must be why the old shaman had called the waterfall "life," for Grandfather had now seen the waters come to life, transcending what he once thought only to be spirit, now was flesh and mind. It was alive in every sense of the word, not just imagination but stark reality, for the mind of the waters had fused with Grandfather's very soul and the communication was profound indeed. It was more than any human lips could convey.

All day long and into the late afternoon, Grandfather kept his vigil on the boulder altar. Though there was no further communication for most of the day, Grandfather had enough to do just trying to digest what he had already learned. Every time he thought of the living waterfall shivers of excitement and gratitude ran up his spine. During the late afternoon Grandfather began to question why this waterfall had hit him so powerfully and seemed so alive. Certainly he had stood before many waterfalls before but none had communicated to him in such a living way. There was always a communication on a spiritual level, but this falls seemed so alive and definitely had a mind of its own. He wondered if in fact all waterfalls were like this one. It may have been that he was just too blind to see the truth before.

He began to think about how all the drops of water and spray combined to make this living waterfall, and how surely they fused to make the streams before and after the falls. It was the collective consciousness of countless parts that made the whole, the grand consciousness, the mind of the waterfall. But where does that collective consciousness begin and where does it end? Is the mind only in this waterfall, or is it in all waterfalls, all waters, and all oceans? Could it be, he wondered, that the consciousnesses of all the waterfalls, the streams, lakes, rivers, and oceans combine to make the grander consciousness, the greater flesh and mind of all waters? After all, all water is connected; even the water of his flesh is connected to all waters of earth and sky.

The sudden realization came over Grandfather that it was not the mind of this particular waterfall, it was not its life solely, but the combination of all waters. This waterfall was a doorway to all other waters and it was all the waters of the earth that Grandfather had communicated with on a living, thinking level. The mere thought of all of this made Grandfather's head spin. It was all so overwhelming. Through this waterfall, through any water, Grandfather could communicate with all waters of the world, even the waters that pulse through the veins of man, animal, plant, and even the rains in the sky. Water then was not just a spiritual entity, but a living, breathing, and thinking being.

Grandfather grew tired from the overload of knowledge and began to slip into a place somewhere between sleep and reality. He wondered to himself if he were not just projecting his own thoughts onto that of the water. But then, he thought, our bodies and minds are composed mostly of water. Is it not then the water projecting thoughts onto itself, using what we consider to be our minds as a vehicle? Are our thoughts really our own, he thought, or are they the combination of many entities, most of which are water? And at what point, he questioned, Do the waters taken into our bodies become living tissue, living brain, our mind? Could the inverse be true, that it is not our thoughts projected to the waters, but the waters projecting their consciousness to us? These questions overwhelmed Grandfather and he fell into a deep and much needed sleep.

He fell into a deep dream, or vision, he did not know which, but the journey seemed so real. He dreamed that he was floating in a vast sea, where no land was visible. He did not feel threatened or afraid of the vastness, instead he felt at peace, part of the whole and not a separate entity. At times he could not feel where his flesh ended and the waters of the sea began. Instead he felt expanded, where his reality reached from shore to shore and touched the very sky. His flesh was that of the ocean and his mind was that of all waters. In one instance he was all waters and yet at the same time could still feel his own identity.

Still firmly locked into the dream or vision he was then lifted from the oceans and began soaring on the back of an eagle. He flew across the waters and a distant land. There he was taken to a waterfall and through that waterfall, like a window, he was instantly connected to all the waters of the earth and sky. He was then taken to a stream, a pond, a river, and a swamp, where there again he felt the connection to all waters. Then he flew to the high mountains and gazed down on the snows, ice, and glaciers, and there again he felt the connection, the mind of all waters. Finally he was taken deep into the cloudy sky, then to the dew-drenched plains, and then to the damp loamy forests, where he again felt all waters. Finally he was flown back to the boulder altar and as he looked into the eye of the eagle, he again was part of all waters. The eagle handed him a pottery cup filled with water, and as he drank he became all water. He awoke to the thunderous roar of the waterfall.

Many questions had been answered in his dream but he did not know how. He had learned, in a very profound way, that any water was like a window through which one could be connected to all waters of the world, no matter what form they took. So too he began to understand the mind and consciousness of the living waters. He understood fully when the waters became living. It was not when the waters entered a plant, a tree, an animal, or man that they became living tissue. For he now knew that water in and of itself is a living, thinking entity. It is always living but its life can only be seen by those who understand first its spirit.

At this point he was overwhelmed by all he had learned of the living waters, but he felt that there was more, much more. Every time he thought of leaving throughout the day, the waterfall would not allow him to leave. In fact, every time that he thought of anything other than what the water had thus far taught him, he was pulled back to the thoughts of living water by the thunder of the waterfall. It was like the waterfall wanted him to do nothing else but to make clear in his mind all that he had learned and make it part of his reality. This process went on throughout the day and well into the evening hours. It was only at sunset that Grandfather became exhausted by all the analysis and he was finally allowed to relax, as if the waterfall said that it was enough for right now.

There was silence throughout the night, not a physical silence, but a silence in further communication with the waterfall. He fell into a deep and dreamless sleep, awakening refreshed at dawn. Again the trembling feeling of anticipation struck him deeply and he knew that he was about to learn more. Yet as he looked to the waterfall he somehow knew that it would not be from the waters this time. This baffled him in a way for he expected that the waterfall would teach him, and again become that window to all waters. But there was nothing but a spiritual silence. Only the anticipation remained as he searched the waterfall for answers.

His attention shifted from the water and he began to gaze at the rock walls that surrounded the waterfall. They were dark and very wet, constantly bathed in the mists of falling water. Strewn randomly across the rocks were patches of ferns, mosses, and other vegetation, sparse nearest to the falling water, but carpeting the rocks farther away. The steep rock walls and the vegetation began to capture Grandfather's imagination with the same intensity he had felt the day before while gazing at the waterfall. Somehow he then knew that the rocks had something to teach him as he felt the beckoning power that the waters had used, now pulling his concentration toward the rocks.

He watched the various birds and small mammals feeding on and around the rock boulders and cliffs. They seemed so at home there, as if their lives were directly connected to the waterfall and the rocks. So too he could plainly see the connection of the waterfall to the rocks and the rocks to the waterfall. Without the rocks, the waterfall could not sing, and without the waterfall the rocks could not be worn away into the soils of the world. One could not live without the other, and suddenly he realized that all other entities of creation could not live without the rocks, the waters, and the very air. He understood then that the rocks were like the waters. The same lessons set forth by the waters were also found in the rocks and, ultimately, the air.

At this point he could feel the rocks, the stones, and the soils of the world moving within his flesh and consciousness. He could feel the connection of these rocks to all other rocks and soils of the world and like the waters, they were all living, thinking beings. They were no longer just spiritually alive, but physically alive. He knew then that the essence of the soil did not come to life only upon entering the plants, but was alive from the very beginning. Like the water, the rocks, the soils, and even the air dwell in their own living consciousness. Combined they become part of the consciousness and flesh of what is classically thought of as the living. Any rock, then, any soil, becomes a window through which all soils and rocks of the earth and sky could communicate. So too was he composed of rocks and air. His consciousness then was not his own, but a combination of rock, air, and water. He was at once connected to all things, part of all things.

Through that dynamic connection Grandfather realized that whatever was done to the soils, the rocks, the waters, and the air of the world, was done also to his flesh and his mind. There could no longer be a separation. Man was soil, air, and water. The combination of all creates flesh, thus the connection can never be broken, but only denied. At that moment, Grandfather felt a kinship to all things, even more than he ever had before. His flesh expanded to include all things, and he never felt so close, so alive, or so real. At this point in his life he was so expanded that he felt the earth moving within him and himself moving within the earth. It was not just his flesh and his mind, but the mind and flesh of all things. And now he knew that he could communicate with all things of the earth and sky through his own flesh, through his inner vision, which in fact was the inner vision of all.

Grandfather stayed at the waterfall for several more days, wandering around the immediate jungle and exploring the upper parts of the falls. He knew that the waterfall was done teaching him, but he was in no hurry to leave the area. He knew that it was the last time he would visit the waterfall in the flesh. He wanted to know it intimately so that it would always remain fresh in his mind. Finally, on the seventh day he departed and headed back up to his homeland, a journey that would take several months. He was drawn again, this time by the lure of Death Valley. A marked contrast exists between this world of water and jungle, and the dry, arid expanses of the desert. There he knew that the lessons of the waterfall would be completed. To understand one, he had to also fully understand the other.

Rick and I could now plainly understand why Grandfather had been so connected to water. It went beyond the sense of thanksgiving and awe. He used any water as a window to all waters. I imagined that when he touched the waters in our camp area, he in fact was also touching that special waterfall of life in South America. It was like a fusion of consciousness, where Grandfather could tap into the entire global water system by just touching the water. So too did I finally understand that to Grandfather, all water was living. It was a single organism of mind and flesh, and not just of spiritual mind as I once thought. From that day on, Rick and I always approached water as Grandfather had done, realizing for the first time that the water was living.

I have always taught my students that the people of the

earth believed that everything had a spirit and thus was alive. They made no distinction between plant and animal, rocks, water, air, and soil. To my students, to me, these things are living before they become flesh. We are the collective total of all parts of earth and sky, a collective consciousness that existed long before we became living. We no longer rush to water in an irreverent way, for we know that we are in fact going back to ourselves, back to our origins, and reuniting with our very blood. In essence, the living waters will be here long after we have become spirit again, and the waters will still contain part of our consciousness as to the rocks, the soils, and the very air. After all, the air we breathe was once breathed by the ancients and the water that has become our blood was once the blood of all living things past.

10

Journey to Death

It was several weeks after we heard the story of the waterfall when Grandfather told us the story of the second half of its teaching, the journey to Death Valley. Ironically, we were walking along the trail we called "Drudgery" heading back to camp when we sat down for a while to rest. Our trek was even more torturous than it had been a few weeks earlier, though the conditions were essentially the same. In fact, I believed that it was a little hotter and drier than it had been on the previous trip, even dustier. The thirst I felt was nothing like I had ever experienced. My lips were so dry that they were cracked. Some of the cracks ran so deep that they would bleed. My throat and lungs were so dry and filled with dust that I could barely cough. There was no moisture left in them to move any of the dust.

Rick and I just lay in the sparse shade along the trail, panting and dizzy. Grandfather, as always, looked so serene. He busied himself with some lizard tracks that stretched across the hot sands and into the low blueberry bushes along the trail. He sat with us, not because he was tired, but to keep us company as we tried to recuperate. I felt like I could not possibly go on, but I had no choice. The camp and subsequently the water were not going to come to me. So too was there no way that I could last out the day and travel at night to the camp. My thirst was just far too intense to linger here for very long. As usual, I paid no attention to any of the marvelous things that were all around me. I was too wrapped up in my pain and thirst. That thirst became like a vacuum that sucked in all my awareness and cast me into a stupor.

Even though I knew that I had no choice but to head back to camp, I still grumbled to myself as Grandfather got up to leave. He walked off with that certain spring in his step that really made me angry. Again, it was not anger at him, but at myself for being so weak and allowing the thirst and pain to rule my life. I wanted to be like Grandfather so much, but I had no idea how to go about changing my attitude toward the intense heat and thirst. Certainly Grandfather had told me many times before that I should not give these things any power over me, but that seemed easier said than done. I was determined at this point, midway through the trek, to find out more about how Grandfather was able to handle the heat with such ease.

As usual, by the time we reached the outer perimeter of camp, Rick and I were running to the water. At this point I still had enough resolve to honor the water and to pray before I dove in, but even my prayers of thanksgiving were rushed. As usual, Grandfather proceeded with his slow approach to the water, the prolonged prayers of thanksgiving, and the touching that connected him to all waters. As usual too, the thirst did not seem to be a factor to him at all, not even an inconvenience. In fact, I imagined that to Grandfather the thirst was kind of a blessing, but I did not know why. To me he looked as if he was rather pleased to be thirsty.

Rick and I lingered in and around the water for the remainder of the afternoon just to regain our strength and to fully hydrate. We did not return to camp until dusk and even then I was still dragging with fatigue. The whole thing was just making me so angry. I again had missed so much because of the smothering encapsulation of thirst. My actions at camp, kicking at stumps and carelessly tossing things about, made my anger very obvious. So too was Rick feeling that same anger. I looked over to where Grandfather was sitting and I was startled to see him looking back at me. He had that smile on his face that told the fact that he knew exactly what I was feeling and he sympathized with my plight. I also knew that smile to mean that he too had gone through the same anger at one time in his life and I suspect that is why he told us the story of Death Valley on this night.

There was not much conversation until later on in the night and then, without any prompting, Grandfather began to speak about what we were feeling. He said, "You are angry at yourself for giving in to the pain, the thirst, and the heat. By giving that pain and thirst power over you, you have seen or experienced nothing other than that thirst. You have cut yourself off from all things because of that power, and you walked as if dead. Yet you knew that you would soon come to water, but you would not release your pain. Instead, you held on to the pain and thirst like old friends. You could not set that aside, even for a few moments. You chose to live in a vacuum of pain, thirst, and, ultimately, self-pity. You could have learned what the thirst was trying to teach, and then let it go, but you would not learn its lessons. Thus you must face the thirst time and time again, until you learn what they have to teach. Only then can you transcend your thirst and remove its power."

I sat in silence for a long time trying to understand what Grandfather was talking about. I had no idea what he meant when he said that I was holding on to the thirst and pain like an old friend. I also had no idea what lessons I was supposed to learn from the thirst. How could anyone learn anything from thirst, other than to appreciate the waters even more? Grandfather's voice broke into my thoughts, saying, "Thirst is a gift to be cherished and understood, for thirst will lead you to a deeper understanding of life. It is only when we can learn the lessons of thirst that we can truly understand life. Thirst is not a demon, but a blessing. It is a reality that is like an island in the world of the unreal."

I sort of knew what Grandfather was talking about, but I had no idea about how to find the deeper lessons. I remembered back to a time when Grandfather was sitting out in front of my house waiting for me. It was a hot, hazy, and humid August afternoon, yet Grandfather sat serenely as usual, with a delighted smile on his face. A neighbor who was passing by asked Grandfather why he never seemed to be affected by either the heat or the cold. I had been amazed at Grandfather's answer. He simply said, "Because they are real." At first I did not understand that answer, but as the months passed I realized the power of what he had said. In a world of a cloistered society, where most living and working environments are unreal and sterile, the reality of nature is a welcome relief. But I still could not understand why Grandfather had said that my thirst was a gift. After all, I did live in the reality of nature and the thirst would not, as far as I was concerned, teach me much more reality. It was then that Grandfather told Rick and me the story of Death Valley.

Grandfather said that soon after he had left the site of the waterfall he knew that he had to go into Death Valley. The thoughts of the trek to the valley grew stronger and more compelling with each passing mile. Even before he had entirely left the jungle, all he could think about were the hot arid deserts. He knew that the lessons learned at the waterfall could not be fully understood until he went to the desert. He instinctively knew that he could not understand the deeper wisdom until he learned the lessons of both extremes. He did not linger long in any one place. Instead, he built camp only when he was forced to replenish his supplies. He traveled for four days, sleeping only on the bare ground, and then would camp for two days, to replenish his supplies. The trek was in fact rushed, driven by the desire to reach the deserts by midsummer.

As he passed through the northern regions of Mexico he did not even consider stopping to see his people. The quest to get to the desert even precluded the visiting of his tribe. Though the urge was there to see old friends again, he knew that he could not veer from his trip. All pleasures of the mind and flesh would have to wait. As he traveled through his homeland, he purposely avoided any possible contact with his people. It was painful at times, but during this whole trek north from the waterfall, pain became his constant companion, and his driving force. At times his pace became so frenzied that he would even travel through the night and most times through the hottest parts of the day, something that was not advisable in desert conditions. He even ran through various parts of the journey, thoroughly exhausting and dehydrating himself even before he crossed the invisible border into the United States.

Finally, after several grueling months of travel at such an inhuman pace, he reached the southern part of the valley. Ironically, he could not go right into the valley. It wasn't so much that he didn't want to, but the valley seemed to be telling him that he would have to wait. This confused Grandfather, especially after such a long and rushed trip to get there. All the while he'd felt as if he were rushing to beat an unseen clock, only to be commanded to wait when he finally arrived. The only thing that he understood without a doubt was that he was not to enter the valley. He decided then to make camp, find food and water, rest, and await for the valley to command him to enter. He felt that it would be a good idea anyway to rest for a while, especially after such a grueling journey. He suspected that was the reason that the valley no longer beckoned.

Several days passed without a sign from the desert valley. Grandfather's strength slowly returned and physically he felt well rested. His spiritual mind, however, would not rest and yearned to enter the valley. It became a struggle to wait, for at times his deepest desires for understanding obscured all other communication. He felt frustrated at times for he knew that some unseen secret awaited him and his anticipation became overwhelming. He wanted to know; yearned to finish the lesson of the waterfall. Finally, on the dawn of the seventh day, the valley called to him again and he knew that he could go in. In a way, it was a relief to finally enter the valley, but he was also a little afraid. He knew that he had to undertake this quest with nothing from the outside world, and wandering alone and naked in the desert would be trying indeed.

This endless track of barren but beautiful wilderness gave him no clues as to where he had to go or what he had to do. Every time, day or night, that he tried to lie down and rest, or gather food, or find water, the call of the desert would not permit him to. He was driven on, part by his own quest to find the answers and part by the very desert itself. With each passing mile he could feel his strength diminishing and his thirst intensifying. Still he pushed on into the heat and cold of the night, his body now racked with pain and his mind near hallucination from lack of water. He began to lose touch with all reality so that all there was, was the intense thirst and pain. Yet his resolve to continue would not diminish. The goal of getting there, no matter where there was, became more important than the pain, even more important than death.

By the beginning of the fifth day, he began to crawl. Walking or even standing became impossible. The sun seemed to burn with more intensity and there was no place of shadow. He crawled on into the most horrible heat of the day, then finally collapsed with fatigue. There was no way he could go on, for now he could not even slide along on his belly. All he could do was to stay right where he lay, unable to move. His quest to find answers, his search for the truth, ultimately led him to the near edge of death. Even though he knew that he was going to ultimately die, he did not care, for all he wanted was to find what he was looking for. If that search cost him his life, then he would not have died in vain. He believed that his life was well worth the effort. As far as he was concerned, if he could not find the answer, then he would rather die.

During this time, as Grandfather was wrapped in a stupor of thought, he failed to notice that the sky was beginning to cloud over. Grandfather was pulled back to consciousness by the feeling of a gentle rain. At first he thought that he might be hallucinating for the first few drops felt like they were burning his flesh. As time passed the rain intensified, but Grandfather did not move. Instead he just lay where he was and cried, though he was so dehydrated that no tears fell from his eyes. It was as if the very desert had seen his desire for the wisdom and given him back his life. He rolled onto his back and felt the gentle rains running into his mouth. As each drop combined and rolled back into his throat, he could feel it fuse with his flesh. There was again no separation from his flesh to that of the waters. The lessons learned at the edge of the waterfall once again came hammering into his mind.

Grandfather knew that the rains would not last long at this time of the year; in fact, they were rare indeed. He worked at gathering as much of the rainwater as he possibly could. He found several shallow basin-type rocks and collected water, all the while keeping his mouth open to the sky as much as possible. He rushed around the landscape, trying to find as many basinlike rocks as possible, but soon to his surprise a large amount of water had collected in a huge tublike depression alongside of a small rock outcropping. He knew instantly that this would be the place where he would set up camp. It was here that the valley wanted him to be. He had shelter and enough water for at least a few days, and food was plentiful. A tremendous sense of relief rushed over him. He felt like he had been reborn from the fires of the desert.

For the next month at least he lived a very Spartan existence. He wandered through the desert whenever he felt moved by the unseen spirit of the valley. Each trek away from the security of his camp, he learned something new, yet there was never a clear communication like that which he received from the waterfall. Even though he had been to the various deserts of the country many times before, he began to learn things that he had never known. The various animals and plants began to teach him small but valuable lessons about life and about living under the harsh conditions of this wilderness. Even the rocks had many things to teach, both on physical and spiritual levels. However, the grand lessons that he came for still would not make themselves manifest. To him the desert seemed to be waiting, but for what he did not know.

Finally, when Grandfather least expected it, he received one of the first grand lessons that the desert had to teach. He was watching a lizard sunning himself in the early morning hours, awaiting the heat to drive away the chill of the night. He admired how easily the lizard seemed to live under such harsh conditions. There was always the possibility of a struggle to live if conditions got bad, but the lizard was part of this whole environment. These lizards were only found in the deserts under these conditions and could not exist in the higher elevations, in the forests, or even in the grassy fields. They needed this place to survive and to live. To them, this place was home and they accepted the torturous conditions without question. The lizards learned to live within the laws of the desert and in so doing, it became home, their only home.

He began, through the wisdom of what he had learned from the lizard, to look into his own life and how he viewed this desert valley. To him, it was not at this point a home,

but still a struggle. He sensed that he might be an alien to
this environment, struggling against its forces rather than
giving in to them. If he could be like the lizard, then this
place would become his home. There would be no struggle,
for if the laws and conditions of the desert are obeyed, then
the desert would truly become home. He began to call this
the philosophy of the lizard, and it was this philosophy that
he wanted to define in his own terms. He wanted to make
that philosophy part of his life so it would direct his actions
while in this place.

Here in the fires of the desert, he learned to appreciate
water to its fullest. Here he could plainly see how every
precious drop of water was so critical to the maintenance
of life. Those lessons were clear, but he still wanted to call
this place home. He felt part of it all, though only spiritually.
He wanted to become part of it through the flesh, as did the
lizard, the various plants, and numerous other animals that
call this place home. The more Grandfather searched his
mind for answers, the more distant he felt from any real
solutions as to how to call this place home. There must be
a key element, a secret of some sort that he had to find. He
resolved himself to solve the secret of the lizard philosophy
and thus solve the question of the desert becoming home.

Grandfather stayed around his camp area for several more
weeks, studying the various wildlife and flora, especially
the lizards, but still there was no clue as to where he could
find the answer. He soon began to exhaust all possibilities
and felt compelled again to push deeper into the desert,
abandoning his camp and his protected but dwindling source
of water. As soon as he thought about it, the feeling of
having to leave immediately overwhelmed him. At first he
thought of wandering back to his camp to take a last drink of
water, but the feeling that he had to leave right away became
very pressing. Without hesitation he wandered again into the
desert, not knowing where he was going, but being driven
definitely to a distant place.

There was never a question in his mind about this compelling force. He had to follow this feeling no matter what
the pain if he ever hoped to find any answers. He knew that
he may have to face death again, but his quest was more
important than his life. Grandfather always believed that if
his life quests were not worth giving up his life for, then

the quest was not worthwhile at all. All too many people go through life dedicated to nothing that they would die for, and to him, that was not really living at all. He had a passion for the things he quested for and in so doing had a passion for living that few others could ever know. The truth, the simple truths of life, was what Grandfather was seeking. His seeking many times would lead him to the edge of death, but it was at this edge that the most profound lessons would be learned. Many times this was the only way they could be learned.

Again he wandered for days, driven beyond pain and thirst to get to some unknown place of wisdom. Again, he was brought to his knees and finally to a state of collapse. Still the desert remained a struggle and except for a spiritual connection, he still felt alien. The pain and thirst were even more intense now than they had been during his first collapse. His body felt as if it were on fire and his throat felt cracked and bleeding like his lips. No clouds could be seen in the sky; there was to be no relief this time. The desert valley had forsaken him and even the spirit world refused to speak. His prayers seemed to fall upon deaf ears and now he felt so alone and rejected. It was almost as if the desert were deliberately trying to cast him out, or even kill him.

He remembered awaking in the night and again in the day. Another night passed, then another day, or at least he thought so. His mind wandered in and out of reality. Time became a myth and place became but a dream. Several times he hallucinated water. At one point in the early morning he felt what he thought was dew on a close rock, only to burn his tongue as he attempted to lick its searing hot surface. He awoke to the feel of stinging rain hitting his back. He at first thought that it was another hallucination but soon began to feel its reality come hammering through to his consciousness. Opening his lips to the sky he began to catch water, and as his strength began to return he began to collect the waters any way he could just as before. Unfortunately, there were no convenient rock catch basins and he had to satisfy himself with drinking as much water as he could hold.

Just at the point where he could not physically hold any more water the rains abruptly stopped and soon after the sky began to clear. It was not long before the sun pounded down on the earth again, turning the desert into an inferno. There

were no rock overhangs where he could find shelter. In fact
there was not much of anything. He was in one of the most
barren places that he had ever been in his life. Squinting
through the wavering lines of heat he could see no areas of
shelter in any direction, no place where he could find safety.
At this point he knew that he had to make a decision. Either
he would have to try to make it back to his original camp
and there find shelter, or he would have to wait here for the
answers to his questions. Ultimately his body would run out
of water, and then he would not be able to make the long
trek back to his original camp.

He searched the sky for answers, but it remained mute.
He sought the spirits for answers, but they refused to speak.
He had to make a decision and fast, either to make the long
journey back to his original camp or ultimately face death.
Simply, he had to abandon his quest and live, or await
answers and possibly die. The urge inside of him was to
go back to the safety of his camp, but he knew that was
not what his spirit wanted. As always, when faced with a
life or death situation, the decision did not take long. He
would rather face the possibility of death than to abandon
his quest. He reaffirmed this decision in his prayers and
almost immediately he sensed something change and shift
deep within him. It was like a sense of knowing something,
but he did not know what.

As if born of some fantasy or dream, he saw a small
lizard disappear under a large flat rock. From his position
the rock appeared to be stuck solidly in the ground but when
he walked over to it, that was not the case. The rock was
embedded in the ground, but only on three sides. In front of
the rock was a deep depression that he could not see from
where he sat. The depression cut deep into the desert floor
and under the rock. It afforded a rather spacious cave, one he
could actually sit up in. To his amazement, the lower portion
of the small cave had collected a good supply of water from
the passing rain. He soon found that it was probably enough
water to last him several days. At that moment he felt so at
peace, so at ease, as if he were nearly home.

He wept at the thought that the small lizard had led him
to this place. The desert was taking care of its own and
through the lizard he had been saved. He was formally
introduced to this desert valley by the lizard and now the

desert would allow him to live a little longer. The desert began to feel more like a home, a place where he actually belonged. Yet, there was still that separation and a piece of the puzzle was still missing. He also did not know why this feeling came over him. It was something felt rather than a conscious thought. It was obvious to him that he had learned a profound lesson, but he wanted to find out why and put it into a language that his mind could understand.

He knew that the metamorphosis of a feeling shifting to thought would not always happen. Many things could be known, but there was no logical explanation attached to that knowing. He realized that he may just have to accept the shift in his perception of the desert and not allow himself the luxury of knowing why. Anyway, the feeling was real enough, for his body and mind now found peace on a deep level. It was not a spiritual change, for spiritually he always felt a part of the desert. It was a definite physical changing of body and mind, small but profound. He sat back in his small cave for a long moment of reflection, pleased at just knowing the change had happened.

Days slipped by as he stayed in and around his cave. He began to see the desert not as a barren and hostile place but a place of infinite life. It was a place not harsh and dry, but a place that took care of its own, on its own terms. Everything that lived and grew in this place belonged here and nowhere else. He too began to feel that he somehow belonged. Certainly he had seen countless living things existing in various desert conditions all of his life, but for the first time he viewed those things differently. He had looked at life on the desert as a constant agonizing struggle for all of its inhabitants, but now he knew that there was no real struggle at all, at least no more so than would be found in any other environment.

All anything that lived here would have to do was obey the laws of the desert. It would have to redefine the terms of survival to fit exactly into the consciousness of the whole, thus the whole becomes living. He began to feel the same wisdom of the waterfall now in this desert valley. The valley, with its torturous heat, lack of water, and emptiness, was actually a living, conscious entity that became part of his flesh and consciousness. Like the waterfall, the desert moved within his flesh and his flesh moved within his body.

There was no inner or outer dimension, no separation of self, just the whole, the oneness of it all. That knowledge became almost overwhelming, too much for him to understand all at once. He reveled in the grand lessons; his outward search of the land became an inward search of the land.

He understood finally that thirst did not mean pain and death. They were the reality of the desert, a gift of life in disguise. It was the intense thirst that led one to survive, like any other instinct. It was the thirst that sharpened the physical and spiritual senses of survival, for the desert allowed no mistakes. The knowledge of thirst thus became the cutting edge of the survivor. The thirst kept one conscious of the frailty of life in this place. Frail yes, but a struggle, no. Grandfather finally understood one of the most basic and precious laws of living with the desert: that thirst is an ally, not an adversary.

From that day on in the desert, Grandfather used his thirst as a guiding force in his survival. Like all the other children of the desert, he began to grow very conscious of water. He began to redefine heat and thirst. They were soon accepted as part of the overall reality, and once accepted they were transcended. They lost their power, for they became a constant part of one's existence here. After all, Grandfather thought, without the heat and thirst there could be no living entity called desert. Like the very desert, in the heat and the thirst he found a certain beauty. The beauty that is part of it all.

As all of these things began to fuse together in Grandfather's mind, he began to understand the desert like never before. With each passing day he felt more and more at home. Old definitions were abandoned and new realities were beginning to make themselves known. Grandfather began to blend his existence into perfect harmony with the rhythms of the desert. Soon there was no struggle in his mind or flesh. He finally belonged, accepting the desert on its own terms and learning to live in balance with its laws. He had nearly died in the desert, but only the alien had died, only to be reborn as a child of this land.

For the first time, Rick and I could clearly understand why Grandfather was not affected by the heat and thirst. It was not that he did not feel them, for he did. He, unlike us, did not fear or fight them, for they were part of the realities of life. He knew them to be precious gifts of life that were a keen driving force in survival. Thirst thus becomes the doorway through which we can see into the heart of the deserts, and more important see into the heart of ourselves. Thirst and heat then are teachers, not purveyors of pain and suffering, but that which frees and enlightens, if we know how to accept and use those gifts.

Certainly both Rick and I had been thirsty many times since. But the thirst had lost its power over us. To us, the thirst no longer prevented us from enjoying, but rather enabled us to enjoy that much more. Every time we were thirsty, we learned from it, especially lessons about ourselves and our perceptions of those things around us. Thirst was a reality of life, one we could accept and redefine as a tremendous teacher. Thirst was real, and we loved everything real.

11

Journey to the Lights

Many months had passed since Rick and I had heard the
story of Grandfather's trek into Death Valley and the impact
of that lesson stayed so strong in our minds. Certainly,
we learned the lessons of heat and thirst, but more so, we
learned that Grandfather never really knew or understood
the desert until that day in Death Valley that he had almost
died. This, in a way, shocked us because Grandfather had
been to the deserts many times before that trek to the valley
of death, yet just being there those times did not guarantee
that he knew the deserts at all, and he was open to learning
more. Most of all it was obvious that Grandfather's many
quests were more important to him than his own life. He
dedicated his life fully to the quest, no matter what the cost.

The lessons of the waterfall and the desert were only part
of the story, however. The final teaching was not to come for
Grandfather until years later when he wandered the farthest
northern reaches of the continent. Only when he finally
faced the northern lights were the lessons complete. Thus,
the lessons of fire and ice, waters and rocks, came to frui-
tion. The ice of the far north held the final key to his search

for what he considered living. It held the wisdom of pure survival without struggle. He had faced the waters of the jungles, the fires of the deserts, and now he had to face the treacherous cold of the north, learning in each instance to accept nature on its own terms and live by its rules. Most of all, each lesson taught him to redefine the consciousness of what was truly living, not just what was spiritually alive.

It was in the dead of winter when we heard Grandfather's story of his trek to the north. We had been living in a survival situation for the better part of a week during our Christmas break from school. We were hit hard by bad weather. It had snowed heavily shortly after we had built our shelters in the earlier part of the week and now the latter half was wrapped in a deep freeze. Rick and I were having trouble functioning at all. We waited until the warmer parts of the day before we would venture out from camp and then not very far. During the morning and through the night, we became prisoners of our fire, unable to go very far except to collect firewood. We had not yet mastered body control and had not fully learned to remove the power from the cold.

As usual, Grandfather seemed to be wholly unaffected by the severe cold. Each morning, without fail, he would go down to the stream to bathe. He did nothing different in the bone-chilling cold that he wouldn't do on a hot summer day. Grandfather was no more bothered by the severe cold than he was with the heat and torturous thirst. I know that he had explained to us many times before the factors involved in his ability to withstand the elements, but I knew that there had to be more. I had seen him use body control to the extent that he could enter chilling waters and actually sweat. He told me numerous times that he would not allow extreme cold or heat to have any power over him. I knew that was but half the answer. His attitude and absolute serenity were such that it transcended even the body control and the power of the cold.

As usual, as we watched Grandfather bathe from the safety of our fire, we both felt so angry at ourselves. I knew that I had a lot to learn about controlling my body and I wasn't sure as to how to remove the power from the storm, but I wanted so desperately to do what Grandfather was doing. I imagined all the wondrous things he was doing and the rapture he was feeling as I huddled close to my tomb of fire. I could see no resistance in his actions, only total acceptance. There was no struggle or fight, not even a goose bump or a small shiver. To me, it appeared as if he were part of the cold and not separated in any way from its power. In essence, he seemed to become the cold and thrive on its power.

The more I watched him, the more determined I became to ask him to give me more answers to the wisdom of the cold. In my mind, the cold was even more powerful than the heat and thirst we had felt on our long summer walk. At least then we could eventually quench our thirst in the waters. Here, the fire was barely keeping us warm. I could not imagine bathing as Grandfather was doing, far less venturing very far from the fire. I became obsessed, overwhelmed, by wanting to know his secret. I suspect, in retrospect, that Grandfather had planned many object lessons such as this. He would coax our curiosity to a point where we wanted to desperately know something. Then, and only then, would he teach us, for he knew that we were then fertile ground for the seeds of wisdom to grow. Our obsession to learn would then drive us through all manner of obstacles.

That night, after a long and cold day of watching him wander about in the cold, he told us the story of his trek to the north country. Shortly after Grandfather left the Death Valley area, he began to feel a calling to wander up the West Coast. It was not a definite call to any specific location at first, but a general feeling of direction. He had been along the entire West Coast several times before, but he suspected that his inner vision was driving him to some unseen lesson yet to be learned. Yet, he felt that there was no rush, not like there had been during his trek from the waterfall to the desert. Instead, he just wandered leisurely, learned, and enjoyed. The only time that any driving force would hit him was when he lingered too long in one place.

He spent several months in the northern California area, alone with the giant trees. He always loved the serenity and wisdom that he found anytime he lived for a while in this area. It was a time for him to relax and be introspective, sorting out the many lessons he had learned during his visit to the waterfall and the valley of death. To him, the trees held unfathomable wisdom and power, wisdom about the past, and, more important, wisdom about the future. He could talk freely and openly to the trees and they to him. As always, he was humbled by their awesome size and power. They were mystical giants that held the wisdom of the ages and could change men's souls. There he purged himself of all the nagging little questions that still haunted him regarding his most recent lessons. There too he grew strong again.

He was beginning to grow content with his camp in the redwoods and, in fact, was thinking about staying there throughout the next season, when the calling to go on hit him again. This time it pulled at him stronger than it had when he first left the desert. Now not only was it giving him a direction, but also a place. He knew that he had to return again to the north country, where the lights dance in the sky. He had been there several years before and spent a good part of the summer season there with a small group of Eskimo people, and now he knew that this was the place he had to go. He was delighted that he would be visiting his friends again, but with the oncoming winter, he wondered how he would survive the trek to their village. So too did he wonder if these people could still be found in the same place. After all, the last time he visited them was in the summer, at their summer camp. He hoped that he could find their winter camp, but resolved himself to allowing his inner vision to guide him.

Grandfather continued his trek up the West Coast, still not in any great hurry. He knew that it would be many months before he even got close to the northern territories and as yet the calling still did not dictate a fast pace. During his journey, he would encounter people who lived along the coast. There he would stay for a while and learn some of their ways and skills. Though he would avoid most encampments and villages, there were a few that he felt he was drawn to. Several of the people along the coast he knew very well for he had visited them many times before and they had become old friends, eager for his company and to share their wisdom. Yet even during his visit with his friends, the inner calling would not permit him to stay for very long. He had to keep going north and there was no doubt in his mind that he would not arrive at his destination until winter.

He knew then that this calling was not only directing him to a particular place but also dictating a time that he had to be there. He found that whenever he tended to rush the trip that his inner vision would slow him down to a point where he just had to stay put for several days. It was almost as if his trip were being solely directed by a force beyond his own will. If he went too fast or too slow, this directing force would make his life miserable. His spiritual mind would not give him any peace unless he followed the directions inwardly given. He learned long ago during his early childhood that it would be almost suicide to go against any of these spiritually directed forces, so he subsequently obeyed them without question or a second thought.

Sometimes these spiritual thoughts directed him to a specific location along his route of travel, as if to prepare him for what lay ahead. One particular incident took him by surprise, especially after the encounter was over. He had been directed far off his route along the Canadian coast. Instead of heading north as the calling originally dictated, he felt a command to go east, far inland. This confused him for a while and he had to camp for several days to make sure that was a true spiritual compelling. He could not understand why, after directing him for so many miles north, the force would suddenly have him change direction. Assured that it was correct, he unquestioningly headed east, deep into the lush coastal mountains.

He traveled for two days but had no idea as to where or why he was going. At times his inner direction seemed to abandon him, leaving him with a deep sense of being lost. Yet, every time he made a slight direction change the force would awaken and guide him back to his original path. He traveled like this for a few days, though the pace was still relaxed and time did not seem to be a factor. However, he felt that he could not tarry for very long in any one camp. He awoke in the morning and was immediately on his way, traveling nonstop until fatigue forced him to camp again. Finally, he arrived in a small valley and he knew somehow that he had arrived. Traveling up the valley, he suddenly came upon a small and very old cabin, nestled along the northern valley wall. It appeared to have been there forever.

As soon as he saw the cabin, he knew that he had arrived at the destination that the inner calling had dictated. At the same time he also somehow knew that this was only an intermediate stop along the path of his greater quest. He approached the cabin carefully. At first glance he could not decide if the cabin was owned by a Native American or some old hermit, such was the way it was built with the evidence of both cultures. He could plainly see a wisp of smoke coming from the old and battered stove pipe so he assumed that someone was living there. He did not want to walk right up to the cabin, for many times people were very protective of their land and did not like strangers. Instead, he approached the cabin very carefully, stopping frequently to try to pick up any evidence of people being about.

He studied the tracks that led to and from the door, from a good distance. He knew then that there was only one person living there and that from the last set of tracks, the occupant must still be inside. He could also tell that the tracks were made by an older man, probably older than he. They also revealed that this man was very aware of what was around him, truly a child of the forest. Yet he still did not know if this old man was from the world of the white man or from the world of the Native American. After a long approach with frequent stops he decided that he could feel no hostility around the cabin. His inner vision told him that there was no real danger so he walked leisurely up to the door.

As soon as he was within five feet of the door an old voice called to him from within the cabin, telling him to come in. It also told Grandfather that he had been waiting for quite a while for him to get there. This startled Grandfather, for the old man had known of his approach long before he had arrived at the cabin. So too did the old one know when he was within hearing distance from the door. Grandfather was surprised at this for very few of the people that he met in his travels possessed any skills that could even come close to the awareness of the old man. Even those people who still lived close to the earth could not come close to what the old man had known through his observations. It was miraculous enough that the old one knew of his approach, but he had done so within the confines and insulation of the cabin. Grandfather was truly amazed as he walked in.

As Grandfather opened the door he saw the old man sitting at a rather weathered and rustic table. In fact, the entire cabin was rustic and hand-hewn. There on the wall was an old musket that looked as if it had not been touched for years. So too were there many handmade items, and most possessed a Native American ancestry. There was little in the cabin from the outside world. It became apparent at first glance that this old man was totally self-sufficient. The old man also fit perfectly into the motif of the cabin. He wore the worn and battered pants of the white race but he also had on high moccasins and a buckskin shirt. His wrinkled and weathered features were that of a white man, but his white hair was long and worn in braids. On his buckskin shirt were several old quill-work designs that were once carefully made but now falling apart with age.

The old man smiled at Grandfather and motioned him to sit at the table. Though Grandfather did not like to be inside cabins or sit in chairs, he did not want to offend the old man. The old one poured some tea into a handmade wooden bowl and handed it to Grandfather with a broad smile. To Grandfather's delight, it was a pine tea and not the typical blend that one would buy from a trading post. Without hesitation, the old man told Grandfather that he was probably from the deep southwest part of the country, guessed his age, and even came close to identifying Grandfather's people. He also told Grandfather that he could see Grandfather was truly a child of the earth and definitely now on a spiritual quest. Grandfather was absolutely speechless at what the old man knew of him. To Grandfather, this old man reminded him of his great-grandfather who had raised him, such was this old one's sense of awareness and keen observation skills.

They talked well into the afternoon. Grandfather was held captivated by the old man's wit, charm, and awareness. It wasn't long before Grandfather also found that this old one was deeply spiritual, knowing many of the things that Grandfather knew about the spirit world. This deeply shocked Grandfather for it was rare indeed for any white man to possess the spiritual skills that this old one maintained. Grandfather felt that this old man was even more attuned to the earth than most spiritual people, and it wasn't long before Grandfather realized that he was in the presence of a white shaman. This was even rarer indeed, for he had never encountered a white shaman before, at least not one of this caliber.

Grandfather exchanged many stories and found that much of their lives were along similar paths. Both were wanderers and searchers, looking for a common truth, a simple truth. Both worshiped the Great Spirit in the temples of creation and there had grown close to all that was natural and spiritual. The old man told Grandfather that in his latter years he had searched desperately for someone to teach, but the world would not listen to what he had to say. Now all he wanted was to live out his remaining years here in the bosom of creation, away from the world of the white man. He was heartbroken that all of his knowledge would die with him and he feared that someday the consciousness of society would destroy the world. The old man felt so helpless in his attempt to try to stop what could be the inevitable destruction of life as he knew it. No one wanted to listen.

Grandfather too felt this way. Many times he would try to teach what he knew but no one seemed to want to learn the old ways or the wisdom of the spirit. He too felt so helpless and he feared that all of his searching, all accumulation of knowledge, would be in vain. Unlike the old man, Grandfather was not going to give up and live alone. He knew that someday, somehow, these old ways of skill and spirit would be passed down. He did not know why, but he felt that the things that he was learning were not only for himself but for the world. The old man had fought a valiant battle to try to pass down what he knew, and he still tried, but now he had grown too old to continue his quest. However, he told Grandfather that he was still learning and would not give up his quest to learn until the Great Spirit took him to the spirit world.

By the end of the day, Grandfather and the old man both felt that they had known each other for decades. Grandfather was truly amazed at the old man's spiritual ability, so too with his spiritual knowledge. He had not met anyone quite his equal in observation and awareness in many years and it was so good to have someone who understood and could talk to him on his own level. Grandfather spent the next several days with the old man, sharing knowledge and learning. They spent many days walking along the various woodland paths around the cabin. Grandfather found that the old man would know where an animal was even before he did. It became a game to them to see who could spot an animal first and farthest away. This contest would keep up from one day to the next and the score would fluctuate frequently. Always at the end of the day it would be a tie score.

Grandfather noticed that the old man did not seem to pay attention to the animal tracks and trails that laced the area. Grandfather thought that this was odd because anyone who was a keen observer of nature and was that aware should also be very aware of tracks. In Grandfather's mind, there could be no separation between awareness and tracking for they were one in the same thing. He just could not understand why so much on the ground was overlooked by the old man. He did not know if it was by choice or accident. He asked the old man why he seemed to pay no attention to the tracks and was struck speechless by the old man's answer. The old man told Grandfather that he had been blind since birth and that the only way he could track was by feeling them with his hands.

Grandfather was truly amazed for there had been no indication in the old man's mannerisms or walk that told of his blindness. It baffled Grandfather that this old man could be totally self-sufficient, so aware, and travel as much as he did in his life in total blindness. Grandfather marveled at the old one's ability, which in fact humbled Grandfather. Grandfather just imagined all the obstacles this old man must have overcome in his life, and how utterly easy Grandfather's quests were compared to the ones this old man had to face in total darkness. Grandfather could not understand why the old man had considered his life such a failure. It was success enough to just be able to take care of himself. He did not have to teach anyone, for he was an inspiration to all, especially now to Grandfather.

The next day, Grandfather prepared to leave the old man. Grandfather told him that he would forever be his inspiration and that he would teach others of what he had accomplished despite being blind. Grandfather said that it would be through him that the old man would see his vision of teaching live, for the lessons that Grandfather had learned from him would forever be part of him and his teaching. Without any good-byes, Grandfather walked away, down the path, and toward the coast once again. There was a sadness, because he knew that he would never see the old man again in the flesh. Certainly, there would always be a spiritual connection, but Grandfather felt that he was losing a father, such was the strength of their friendship and love. Tears filled Grandfather's eyes as he waved a last good-bye from the distant trail. He smiled when the old one waved back, knowing without seeing that Grandfather had waved. He was held in awe once again.

Within a few days, Grandfather was at the coast again and heading north. Still his trek was not rushed, but the calling still guided him. He wondered to himself about the deeper lessons he had learned from his visit to the old man. He knew that there had to be more than just the inspiration the old one had been. After all, the directing force that he was following led him there for a reason and he knew that it had to be more than was obvious now. Though as much as he searched his heart, the lessons were not yet apparent. He knew he would have to resolve himself to accept what he had learned and allow the rest to emerge as it was meant to. Still, the thoughts of the old man would not leave him. Each time a certain sadness would follow but he did not know why.

Several days had passed since Grandfather had left the old man's cabin and thoughts about him diminished. One night, as Grandfather slept by his open fire, he had a dreamlike vision of the old man walking up the mountain. He could plainly see the old one nearing an upper ridge, a ridge that was composed entirely of light. In his dream the old man turned to look back down the trail he had taken. Grandfather saw him smile at him for a moment, wave, and then walk into the light. Grandfather awoke with a start, sweating and trembling from the vivid impact of the dream. At once, he knew that the old man's vision was finished and instinctively he knew that the old one had died. The loss he felt was so overwhelming that he sobbed for a long time, until dawn's light dried away his tears.

Could it be, Grandfather thought, that the old man was kept alive just long enough to pass something on to him? Now that the wisdom was exchanged, it was time for the old one to take his final walk to the light. Grandfather felt humbled by this thought, for though there was no evidence for what he felt, the old one seemed desperate to pass on his knowledge to Grandfather. Again he wished that he knew what the deeper lessons were. Without truly knowing if he may be dishonoring the old man's vision, he swore to himself that he would try to understand all the lessons that the old man had passed down to him. To give nothing less than his full attention to those known and unknown lessons, Grandfather would only defile the old man's life and memory.

For the next several days, Grandfather decided to camp and devote his full attention to the old man's teaching. He actually went against the directing force that was pushing him northward, for he felt that the lessons were more important right now. He did not feel that he could go on until at least he had tried to find the deeper lessons. The driving force kept pushing him harder and harder as he lingered and thoughts of the old man grew more faint. Eventually, he could not concentrate on the old man's vision for very long without being distracted by the calling of the north. It was as if he had to go on or the calling would not let him think at all. It was on a walk in the misty morning hours that Grandfather saw the old man standing on a distant northern ridge, beckoning him to come. He knew that now the old man called him again to the north and he had to go without knowing the secret of the old man's vision.

By the time Grandfather was halfway through Alaska, winter was setting in. Still, the voice was calling him onward, to go farther north. This began to frighten Grandfather for he knew that he would eventually get into the tundra area where the trees ended. With the ever deepening snows, this would be a struggle. At best it would be very difficult to build any kind of permanent survival camp. Temperatures would be at killing level and he could make no mistakes for even a slight miscalculation would certainly cost him his life. Still he obeyed the calling to go on even though he knew that it might mean his life.

In the final days the calling pulled at him stronger, now rushing him along his journey. It would permit him very few rests and his camps were now always rushed. There came a point where he could not go onward without snowshoes and it took him several days to make them. The whole time the calling voice nagged at him to hurry. Finally, after what seemed to be an endless trek, he came to a place where the calling subsided, then disappeared altogether. He knew then that he was where he was supposed to be. There was no question, though he did not know yet why he had been led to this place, nor what lessons were about to be learned. He just busied himself making a permanent camp, before the land was fully locked into winter's grip.

His camp was located midway along a finger of timber that reached out into the tundra. It was the last place trees could be found, and the only place he could safely camp. Anything out on the far reaches of the tundra would be suicide. Within a few days he realized that it was not the tundra that he camped near, but along the shores of a frozen and snow-covered lake. The tundra lay far beyond and to the northern horizon. Yet he knew this was the place he had been directed to, without a doubt. So too was the task of survival made easier for him. In the forest where he chose to camp there was an old broken-down hunter's cabin and with a little patching, it made a warm shelter. In fact, it was more of a shelter than a cabin, made almost entirely with crude tools and lashed together with rawhide.

Grandfather spent the next several days collecting food and firewood before the furious storms of winter locked him in. So too would the deeper snows cover almost all food sources, so he had little time for anything else than to gather and repair. Usually he was so tired when he was done for the day that he slept solidly. No thought was really given as to why he was there or what he was going to do when he was finished his preparations for the day. He was in a dead race against the oncoming of severe cold and heavy snows and there could be no time to relax and be introspective. That would be a luxury he could not afford. Very few people lived this far north and those who did had long since prepared for the oncoming season. He felt so alone and isolated in his struggle.

As his camp began to take shape and all the chores of putting food by were taken care of, Grandfather finally had time to relax and enjoy the frozen landscape around him. He began to observe the local wildlife and marveled at how easily they seemed to survive. The ptarmigan were of special interest. To him, these birds looked totally unconcerned and unaffected by the severe cold weather or the deep snows. They needed nothing for a bed other than to burrow right into a snowdrift and become part of its whiteness, totally safe and camouflaged from everything. He marveled at these little birds and how frail he seemed in comparison. After all, they needed nothing to survive here for they were part of these frozen lands. He on the other hand needed all manner of food and tools to barely scrape out an existence.

As the days slipped by, he knew that the ptarmigan of the frozen places were like the lizards of the deserts. Both belonged and both were part of it all. He began to accept the frailties in himself, resolving himself to the fact that man needed tools to survive. Unlike the ptarmigan who needed nothing to survive here, he needed everything and somehow that always made him feel alien to this place. It was depressing to Grandfather to think of himself as being an alien to all places because of the need to make tools. Realistically, he thought, the only place that a man could survive without making anything would be in only the warmest and lushest places of Earth Mother. At that moment, though he felt a certain peace about living in such a cold place, he still felt a little removed and alien. He so wanted to be part of things, like the ptarmigan were to the frozen places and the lizards to the deserts.

He spent days exploring his little stand of trees, the frozen lake, the snow-covered hills, and the tundra beyond. He found that even though he still felt like a poor survival risk and an alien, there was no struggle. As he had learned on the desert, he had to obey the laws of the frozen tundra and become part of that law. It delighted Grandfather to know that he had taken the lessons of the deserts and now applied them to this wilderness. Here he looked again at the whole as a living entity, not just spiritually alive but physically alive. By understanding the consciousness of this place, he became part of that consciousness, and by doing so his mind was also composed of the ice, snow, and cold. He felt closer, but still he wished to be as the ptarmigan.

What confused Grandfather was that he did not know why he had been led here to the tundra. There was no struggle and he easily accepted the living consciousness of this wilderness. He knew that there had to be more, but the lessons at hand were not as clearly defined as were those of the lizards of the desert. He began to grow impatient, feeling that he should possibly struggle before he arrived at any future answer. Yet the thought of making this into any kind of a struggle seemed impossible. At this point, everything was so easy. The only thing he could possibly do was take a vision quest, but even that would not be all that difficult. Somehow he knew that the answers must lie in the wisdom of the ptarmigan though he did not know how to find that wisdom.

One night he was drawn out into the center of the lake. He sat there on the edge of a frozen snowdrift for a long time, gazing out into the distant sky. The northern lights danced their intensity like he had never seen before. They illuminated the entire lake making everything dance with their own play of light and shadow. He gazed at the sky, held in awe. The beauty was almost unbearable and tears began to fill his eyes. Suddenly, this barren and frozen place became more alive than he ever imagined. He took notice of the blowing snows gathering around him and the deep cold. He soon became part of the drift, never taking his eyes from the dancing sky. He felt so alone, wishing that he could share this magic with the world. The isolation of this far northern lake filled him with sadness, for this show would truly go unseen by anyone, even many of those who called this place home.

It was then, when he felt so alone and isolated, that he noticed a tiny little glistening black dot in the snow next to him. He could see the reflection of the northern lights glistening in this little dark pool of waterdrop. He stared at it for a long time, trying to decide if the image was real or imagined. Then it moved slightly and he found that the little dark pool seemed to be looking back at him. He suddenly realized that he was looking into the eye of a ptarmigan that was nestled in the snowbank right next to him. Like him, the ptarmigan was watching the northern lights and watching him. The feeling of aloneness and isolation suddenly dropped away. In the eye of the ptarmigan, he knew a friend, a searcher of beauty and simplicity, like himself. The ptarmigan was also finding unspeakable beauty in the lights and a bond was forever formed between them.

Grandfather wandered back to his camp wrapped deep in thanksgiving for the lesson shared by the ptarmigan. He now felt as if he were accepted by this place, though as he reached his shelter the feeling of being an alien returned to him. His shelter appeared to him as that which separated him from this place and the "oneness" he wished to achieve. He longed to be able to do what the ptarmigan had done. It was then that he remembered something the old blind man had shown him, a lesson that fulfilled the reason for his journey here. It was the image of the ptarmigan's eye that made him think of it, a ptarmigan's eye that he had seen once before with the old man. At the time the lesson did not seem all that important, but now its full impact came hammering home.

Grandfather remembered walking in the woods near the old man's cabin when they came upon a dead ptarmigan. The old man said that a friend of his had tried to raise ptarmigan but the attempt became futile and many of them escaped from captivity. The old man told Grandfather that these birds could not survive in this part of the world because they needed the cold tundra areas. The old man told Grandfather that he had found most of the birds dead during the past summer. Grandfather remembered looking into the frosted eye of the dead ptarmigan feeling a sense of loss and sorrow. He knew that the bird was out of his element and survival for him would be nearly impossible. The bird was truly alien to this landscape and weather conditions.

Grandfather suddenly felt elated because a big question had been answered through that ptarmigan. All of this time Grandfather understood that mankind was a poor survival risk, and because he needed his tools he was alien. But now, Grandfather saw the need for these tools not as a liability but as a blessing. It was through the tools that man could go anywhere he wanted, enjoying the splendor of nature. He was not confined and alienated from any place, but as long as the rules were obeyed, free to wander like so many other animals could not. No, it did not make Grandfather feel above the animals or the laws of creation, but finally it made him feel like part of it all. Yes, man's need for survival tools were still a liability but at the same time, a blessing. As long as the rules were obeyed, then man would not be alien. As long as he understood the living consciousness of the land, there would be no struggle.

Within a few days, Grandfather left his arctic camp and the wisdom of the ptarmigan and headed back to the coast and eventually south. He wandered for many months, now with no real driving purpose other than to explore. It felt good to him to have a reprieve like this from the learning and searching process, especially from that driving voice that had been with him for over two years. As he wandered back along the coast, the driving force hit him again, calling him once again to go inland. Without a doubt, Grandfather knew where the voice was telling him to go. He was headed to the old man's cabin again, yet he knew in his heart that the old man would not be there. At least he could pay homage to the place and honor the old man's memory in prayer and ceremony.

It took several days to get to the cabin and to Grandfather's surprise there was smoke coming from the old chimney. The place definitely looked as if it was still lived in. Grandfather quickened his pace and walked right to the cabin door. Even before he could knock, a voice told him to come in. It was not the old man's voice but a younger voice, yet it contained the same sense of knowing and awareness as had the old man's. Grandfather opened the door to find a young man sitting at the table. He wore buckskins that had been decorated with quill work. He smiled up at Grandfather and told him to sit down. Grandfather was held spellbound by this young man for he seemed to have many of the mannerisms and much the same awareness as the old man.

Grandfather stayed with the young man for several days. To his amazement, the young man, called Ben, was the great-nephew of the old man. Ben told Grandfather that he used to spend many summers in this place, but the lure of the city had taken him away for a while. He said that his search had now brought him full circle and he wanted to follow in his great-uncle's footsteps. He wanted to preserve and pass on the old one's vision. Grandfather realized then that the old one's vision was now living and he had gotten his wish. On the day that Grandfather left, Ben said that he had a gift he had to give him from his great-uncle. With that Ben handed Grandfather the feathers of a ptarmigan and said that his uncle had told him that Grandfather would know what they meant. Tears filled Grandfather's eyes as he walked away.

I looked at the ptarmigan feathers in Grandfather's braid and finally understood their significance that had eluded me for such a long time. Rick and I were held spellbound by

Grandfather's story. No, it did not make it easier to take the cold of this night but it did open up a whole new way of thinking about man and nature. I too had seen the tools of survival as a liability, but now looked at them as a blessing. So too was I beginning to reconsider what I thought to be living and nonliving. Everything had a living consciousness, the sum of all its parts. I too was part of that consciousness. That night the fire no longer felt like a prison, but that which freed us to enjoy this place.

12

Broken People

I remember traveling so often to the far western edge of the Pine Barrens to visit one of Grandfather's old friends. This man, who Grandfather called Half Tree, was of Native American ancestry, though I had no idea as to which tribe he belonged. He lived deep in the woods, without plumbing or electricity, and generally kept to himself. It seemed that he had once lived in the confines of society but was met with prejudice and rejection through much of his early life. He decided long ago to get as far away from people as possible and live as much as he could from the earth. He seemed to be an old broken and bitter man who rarely smiled. Grandfather seemed to be the only one he really trusted and I could not tell if it was because of Grandfather's power or the fact that he was also Native American.

Half Tree never paid much attention to Rick and me. In fact, I believed that he only tolerated us because of Grandfather. Though I had done nothing in the past to upset or bother him in any way, he seemed to hold me in the most contempt. Any conversation with him was always dealt in a very sarcastic way. When Grandfather was not around,

181

he did not talk to me at all. I could sense a deeply hidden hatred in him, but I could not figure out why. After all, how much more could he want? He was living close to the wilderness and away from society. He seemed to have everything he needed and he seemed to love the woods. I could not understand why he was always so unhappy. I don't think that I had ever heard him laugh, and rarely would he smile, even for Grandfather.

Grandfather seemed, however, to understand what was bothering Half Tree. I noticed that the two old men would talk for hours and when they were done, Half Tree seemed much more at peace. It was during these times that he would sometimes smile, and that made me think that somehow Grandfather was helping him through what had tormented him. As the months slipped by, I could see a definite change in Half Tree. He smiled more often and would even talk to me. After a while he would come to me and ask me a question about a skill that he was learning from Grandfather. He seemed genuinely appreciative of all that we taught him. In fact, he learned the old skills with a greater passion than I had ever seen before. Even in the woods he now seemed more at peace, and often I would hear him and Grandfather laugh over something. The change became remarkable, to a point where I could not believe that the old Half Tree and this Half Tree were in fact the same person.

As the months passed and the improvement in Half Tree became more dramatic, my curiosity began to get the better of me. I wanted to know what the original problem was that had tormented Half Tree. He seemed to carry a deep hatred and even appeared to be wrapped in self-loathing at times. So too did Half Tree seem to be haunted by some unseen secret that he suffered through by himself. I knew very well that Grandfather possessed the ability to heal, but what he had done for Half Tree was a miracle as far as I was concerned. Since I was so interested in the "medicine ways" of healing and had helped Grandfather so often collect the healing herbs, I decided to ask Grandfather how he was able to help Half Tree.

Grandfather said, "I was able to help Half Tree because I once felt as he did. I was as broken and bitter inside as was he. But I learned to heal myself, and thus was able to heal him." Grandfather told me that Half Tree was suffering the same pain as were so many of the Native people. They had been imprisoned, their culture destroyed, their lands stolen, and they were not allowed to practice their skills or religion. Their families were torn apart and they were forced to live the way of the white man, away from the earth. They were taught that their ways were primitive and wrong, that their religion and way of life were wrong, and they would have to learn to live like the whites. They were hated and scorned, looked upon as no better than white man's animals, and thus their spirits were broken. It was then that Grandfather told me his story of pain.

As Grandfather first began his long journey in life, he would slip on and off of the reservations unobserved. He was hoping that he would be able to find people to teach, people who wanted to learn the old ways. Though he found many willing students at first, he found that they would not stay with him for very long. They feared reprimand from the white man for learning and keeping alive the old ways. He found that more often than not he was dealing with a broken and imprisoned people, people who had seemed to have lost all hope and even belief. There he found poverty and starvation. The officials seemed to be corrupt and the people lived in appalling conditions. Punishment was frequent and savage and the people seemed to live in a perpetual fear. Many could not even practice their religion freely.

Children were quickly taken from their families when they reached school age. They were sent away to distant schools for reeducation and sometimes never saw their families again. The land that they lived on was not productive and they had to rely solely on the white man for supplies. The psychological warfare and brainwashing that these people were subject to was even more appalling than the conditions that they lived under. There was no peace to be found. The conditions were crowded and many times the white man would pit one tribe against the other, even in the confines of the reservation. Disease and starvation were killing more of these people than any war ever had, and alcohol was becoming an escape for many.

It was on one of these journeys into a distant northern reservation when Grandfather was almost caught by a white patrol. He hid at the edge of a swamp, partially buried in the mud, for several hours as the patrol watered their horses and ate. As the patrol finally began to saddle up and leave the area, Grandfather heard a stirring from the edge of the swamp, not far from where he lay. He knew that it must be the movement of a man, for it was too loud and erratic to be that of an animal. The men on horses took notice of the sound too and began to head in the direction of the sound. As they got closer to the origin of the noise, Grandfather heard a splashing moving quickly toward him. Whoever originally made the noise was now escaping in his direction, and rather loudly too.

The low brush parted and a young Native American man crawled through on his belly. The patrol was searching the area of the original noise frantically and as the young man crashed through the brush in front of Grandfather, the patrol began to head his way. Without thinking, Grandfather reached up and grabbed the young man by the arm, covering his mouth with his hands and pulling him into the mud. The young man struggled at first, but upon seeing Grandfather's face, he gave in to the mud. The men were closing in on the area fast, but would not venture out from the hard bank. Grandfather picked up a small stick from the brush clump and deftly tossed it into a clump of grasses not far from where they lay. A duck took flight in a sputter of whipping brush and flying water. The men of the patrol laughed, then abandoned their search, figuring that it had been the duck that had made the noise. Within moments they were riding out of sight.

Grandfather pulled the young man from the mud and they washed off in the water without a word. The young man looked at Grandfather in amazement, scrutinizing his buckskin clothes. The young man was definitely Native American but he wore the clothes and shoes of the white man. He seemed to Grandfather to be a little ashamed of the way he was dressed. Grandfather, seeing the way the young man was eyeing him, said, "You look like you have seen a ghost." The young man retorted with a sound of amazement in his voice, answering, "Maybe a ghost from the past, old one. I didn't think that anyone like you still lived. I cannot believe how easily you helped me to escape the patrol." Grandfather and the young man laughed long and hard at the surprise on the men's faces when the duck flew off, and that laughter seemed to put the young man at ease.

Grandfather and the young man sat on the bank and talked through much of the day. He found that the young man did not have a Native name but was called John, and he lived on the reservation not far from where they sat. He told Grandfather that the reason he was hiding from the patrol was that he was trespassing on private lands and this area was off-limits to everyone on the reservation, including the elders. He explained that the reason he was here was not to steal cattle as the white men suspected, but to locate a sacred place that the elders so often spoke of. He said that it was hard to find these places anymore, as most of the elders who knew of the old ways were dead or were very old. Many of the elders feared reprimand from the whites and would not openly discuss the old ways.

John told Grandfather that he was trying to preserve what he could of the old ways that would soon be lost forever, most of all the wisdom of the religion of his people. He told Grandfather that many of the young men and women had gone off to try to live in the cities; some too had volunteered as soldiers in this Second World War that was going on. He also said that many had turned to alcohol and lived at the edge of starvation in slumlike conditions. Many of his people had lost their will to live and the spirit of the tribe had been long since broken. He told Grandfather that he had tried to go outside the reservation to make a living but there he was not fully accepted in the white society. He was ridiculed and hated; prejudice and mistrust ran wild. He had felt less than human. Only his search to save the old ways provided a sense of self-respect.

John begged Grandfather to tell him his story. Grandfather briefly told of his quest and his life and how he too had sought to preserve the old ways. He told John how difficult it had been to find anyone who would listen to him and how he felt like many of these old ways would die with him. As Grandfather finished his story a huge smile of satisfaction came over John's face and he began to beg Grandfather to teach him. He said, "I have prayed for someone like you to come and teach me for so very long. I was beginning to lose faith that the Creator wanted to preserve these old ways." Grandfather smiled at John, seeing his enthusiasm, and told him that he did not have to beg. Grandfather would be willing to teach anyone who would listen. As darkness overtook the land, John wandered back to the reservation and Grandfather stayed by the stream. They would meet at the same place the next day.

For many weeks that followed, John would meet Grandfather every morning by the stream. Grandfather first taught him how to survive with nothing, allowing the earth to provide while obeying her laws. He also taught him how to track, even over solid rock. Lessons in awareness and stalking occurred almost every day without fail, and intertwined with it all was the philosophy of living with the earth. After several weeks of training in the physical skills, Grandfather began to teach John the spiritual ways. Here too John was quick to learn whatever Grandfather taught, remaining open to all of Grandfather's philosophies. John was a fast and eager learner, and often begged Grandfather to teach him more than he could handle. Grandfather too got much from teaching John. For the first time in his life he felt a hope for the people of the earth, and John was the embodiment of that hope.

John's love and excitement for the skills must have filtered back to the reservation for after a while John began to bring back other young people who wanted to learn. Though the young men and women he brought back with him were not as eager to learn as John was, they were still at least interested. These people too gave Grandfather even more of a sense of hope for the future. However, it perplexed Grandfather that he had not been invited to the reservation. John and the others who had come to him always seemed to be sneaking away to see him. They were sensitive of their movements and always seemed so hypervigilant for any sign of a patrol. It was obvious that they did not want to be seen by either the patrols or by certain people on the reservation.

Bothered by the fact that he could not go to the reservation, Grandfather finally confronted John over the reason he had to remain a secret. John told Grandfather that not everyone in the tribe could be trusted. There were some who were corrupt and close to the white man. If they found out that some of the young people were going back to the old ways, there would surely be repercussions in one form or another. Grandfather thought it very sad that some of the tribe could not be trusted; he wondered how many other traditions of brotherhood had been beaten out of the people. He could see that many of the people were deliberately turned against each other, creating a mistrust. This mistrust would keep people from openly saying anything about the conditions they lived under, a definite sign of psychological warfare.

Upon Grandfather's urging, John finally took him into the heart of the reservation, but at first only under the cover of night. In all the times he had ever visited a reservation he had remained only on the outskirts, never in their centers of population. Nothing in his past could prepare Grandfather for what he was about to see in the visits that followed. He found the conditions deplorable. Many dwellings were nothing but poorly made boxes without floors and no internal heating. There were no real sanitation facilities, running water was rare, and only a few of the houses had electricity. Garbage lay everywhere. Truly, the white man had reduced these once proud people to animals.

Soon, Grandfather was introduced to numerous "trusted" people by John. Here Grandfather could see how the horror had spread even into the souls of people. He was horrified to see these once proud people who lived so close to the earth now battered, imprisoned, and broken. He saw people who lived in constant fear of each other and the white man. Most of all, the people seemed to have lost all hope. It was at this point that Grandfather began to sense a tremendous loss. The people of the earth were being wiped out right before his eyes and he stood by helpless. Though his people still remained free, these people were his people too. Depression and pain washed over him as he saw, and finally understood, the oppression of the white man.

Grandfather stayed at the edge of the reservation for several more weeks. Most of his students had lost interest in what he was teaching or moved on to something else. John remained extremely interested, but finally moved on to teach at another reservation. In John, Grandfather saw his hope stay alive. John was going to work in the reservation school and hopefully teach the children some of the old skills and the ways of the spirit. As Grandfather began to wander back to the Southwest, he could clearly see that the battle that lay ahead for John was immense indeed. It would seem almost impossible that one lone man could affect any kind of hope or change. Grandfather's heart was also heavy with sadness and depression. He felt that he was one of the only ones left who was free to practice the old ways. He was alone.

During his trek back to his people, Grandfather became wrapped in the deepest depression of his life. His sense of being alone, of loss, became overwhelming at times. He knew that there were elders on all reservations that still lived in the old ways, but his main worry was the future generations. White man's brainwashing and his plan to acculturate the Native Americans were affecting the thinking of the children and the young adults. The old ways were looked upon as primitive and the children were ridiculed for showing any interest in them. Sometimes children would be openly punished for seeking the old ways. The lure and empty promises of the white race were further removing the children from the path. There was little hope in Grandfather's life at this point and he became very bitter.

Grandfather began to see himself as imprisoned, though not as it was on the reservations. He could not really be a free man to go and come as he pleased. He could not wander as did his ancestors. He was restricted, for he always had to take great care in his travels so as not to be seen. He could not travel in the open, but had to most times confine his movements to the thickets or the cover of night. He had to remain always vigilant and aware of possible danger. This thought and realization began to imprison his soul and he felt the pain that many people on the reservations felt. He felt his faith shaken and his spirit breaking. He began to imagine again that many of the old ways would probably die with him, for all hope seemed lost.

Feeling now the huge impact that the loss of the people of the earth would be, he began to feel a certain self-loathing begin to erupt. He began to wonder to himself if his ways were wrong and the white man was right. He wondered if his primitive ways were indeed only for backward people. How could all those white men be wrong? After all, all people that lived close to the earth were now imprisoned. If the Native people were right, would it not be the white man who lived on reservations? If the Native people were close to the Creator, then they would have been able to drive the white man back to the sea from which he came. Self-doubt began to affect Grandfather's every thought, and the depression became oppressive and overwhelming. Grandfather just wanted to go back to his people to die. He could see no sense in trying to teach for it now seemed a lost cause with no hope.

Grandfather camped for many days just outside the perimeter of his people's encampment. He could not face them with the way he was feeling. Though his people still lived wild and free and practiced the old ways, this was but an illusion. His people were as restricted and imprisoned as he. They were old now, with no young blood to pass on the skills to. They were a dying clan, a clan of the old ways, with no one to teach. He did not want to go to them bearing the spirit of bad news, or tell them that they were among the last. In their latter years he felt that it would be best if they continued to live believing that there were other wild and free tribes roaming the wilderness. He had to wait before he faced them so that he could compose his thinking.

One morning as he sat in his sacred area and prayed, Coyote Thunder came to him. Grandfather was startled to see him standing there. Without waiting for Grandfather to speak, Coyote Thunder said, "We knew many days ago that you were coming. We also know what troubles your heart, for I too have seen the pain of broken spirits. That is why I will not allow the people of the clan to get too close to the white man. Instead we prefer to remain hidden until our final days. You now see no hope, but there is hope. You must teach anyone who will listen. The things of truth and spirit will never pass away, but prevail in the end. They will always be part of those who seek the earth and walk close to the spirit. Teach all who seek the earth, no matter race or belief, for those who seek the earth will become the new children of the earth. Our ways will not die. In the final days, man will seek again the things that we know."

Coyote Thunder walked away in silence, giving Grandfather no chance to speak. He could feel a renewed sense of hope arising within him. He knew that it was his vision, his destiny, to teach and he now knew that he should try to teach anyone who would listen, whether Native American or white. He knew that Coyote Thunder was right. The old ways and philosophies would not die. As the white man eventually saw the emptiness of his ways and the numbness of the flesh, then these ways would be reborn. He had to pass them down so that when the white man began to search beyond the flesh, he could find a way. Without hesitation now, and with a renewed sense of hope, Grandfather went back to his people and awaited his next journey, his next student.

I could now understand what Grandfather had given to Half Tree. He had given him hope, possibly for the first time in his life. I am sure that Half Tree had felt the same way as did all people imprisoned on a reservation, knowing that he was one of the last of a people. Humiliated, ridiculed, and broken, Half Tree could do nothing but hate himself. After all, that was what the white man had led him to believe. I could also begin to identify with Grandfather and Half Tree. After all, I was seeking the old ways of skill and spirit. I was imprisoned by a white society that would not allow me to practice what I lived and believed. I felt ridiculed, scorned, and treated like an outsider by many of my friends. I was more like Grandfather than I could ever imagine and from that day, Half Tree and I became brothers.

13

To Teach

In everything he did, Grandfather seemed at peace with a life filled with joy. However, he seemed the happiest when he was either involved in helping someone to heal, or when he was teaching. He loved to teach more than anything else he did. He would go out of his way to create an opportunity where he whet our appetite for a skill, then make us coax him to teach us. He would hold back just long enough to make our interest in a skill so intense that we wanted nothing more than to learn that skill. He would first create a need within us to know and then fill that need when our interest and drive was at the highest. He would not teach us anything that we did not desperately want to know and it was he who first would create that desperation. We had to want to know something very badly before he would open up.

So too was Grandfather a "coyote teacher." A coyote teacher was not someone who would lay out everything for a student, giving him all the answers and techniques. Instead, a coyote teacher was one who planned a lesson so that the student would have to think, make mistakes, and then find the answer by himself. It was not an easy way of learning, but a far superior way to learn. Once a skill or technique was mastered in this way, the student had not only learned the skill fully, but mastered that skill for almost every situation that would arise. I suspect that Grandfather learned to teach from the way he was taught. Hearing the many stories about the way Coyote Thunder had taught Grandfather, I look back and see many of those same lessons passed down to me in the same way.

In all the years I was with him, I never saw Grandfather tire of teaching. I know at times he would be exhausted from a long day of hiking, but as soon as we showed any interest in something he would snap out of his fatigue and eagerly teach us. Our enthusiasm seemed to buoy him up and he found a certain deep satisfaction in watching us learn. There was never a wrong time to ask Grandfather a question. Teaching was all he wanted and was the greatest quest in his world. Even in the most dire teaching situations he would never lose his sense of humor or tire of the task. This teaching attitude bothered me a bit because I too wanted to teach. However, the few times I had tried to teach someone seemed such hard work and I would become frustrated so easily. I asked him one day how he could remain so enthusiastic about teaching all of the time, without getting tired and frustrated. That is when he told me the story of his quest to teach.

Shortly after leaving the reservation and rejoining his tribe, Grandfather began to get the calling again to go out and wander. This calling, however, was more a directive to teach than to go out and seek some spiritual enlightenment. For many months he had the intense, almost overwhelming feeling to teach, but he did not want to go. He had been so frustrated with his teaching attempts in the past that he really wanted nothing to do with it at the moment. He still felt injured spiritually from his visit to the reservation and deep inside he felt that he would only encounter the same pain when he went out again to find a student. The people of his clan now were very old and very experienced, so there were no teaching opportunities where they were concerned. Their skills were impeccable.

What bothered Grandfather the most was that in all of his teaching experiences of the past, they were all short-lived. It seemed that his students would stay with him only for a few months or a few seasons and then go on to do something else. He could never fully finish what he wanted to teach, for that would take years. It seemed to him that adolescents and adults had too much else to do with their lives than learn the old ways. He knew that if he were to ever pass along what he knew, he would have to find a younger student, someone who had a passion for learning that would exclude all else, and would give Grandfather the years he needed to teach fully. He knew that finding such a student would become the biggest quest of his life. Now that he was growing old, he was running out of time and he began to fear that his vision would never be passed down. All would die with him.

The intensity of the deep spiritual drive to go out and teach hammered at Grandfather every day. It gave him no peace, only torment. The torment grew stronger the longer he put off his departure. Still he stalled, trying to figure out first where he should go and what he should do. In his heart he thought this time would be his last time to find a student. His years were now numbered and he no longer had the luxury of time. He knew that he would have to find someone soon and the longer he delayed the more impossible it all seemed. Finally, unable to take the spiritual torment anymore, he left his people again. He had no idea as to where he was going, but he had to go someplace and at least try to fulfill his vision.

Grandfather knew that he would willingly teach anyone who would listen to him, but he also knew that he would have to find someone very young with plenty of time and a passion to learn. This would be the only way he could pass down all that there was. However, he knew that the greatest obstacle would not be the finding of such a person; after all, all children seemed to like what he taught. The problem would be with the society they lived within and their parents' fears. Though the reservation life now was becoming more open and relaxed, many parents wanted their children to learn the ways of the white man so that they could become a success. They still looked at the old ways and skills as primitive, something that was no longer needed. Still, Grandfather thought his greatest hope lay in teaching on the reservations.

He decided, more by thought than with his heart, to go and find John, the young Native man he had taught years ago. He knew that John had moved to another reservation with the hopes of teaching the old ways to the children. Grandfather thought that if he could find John, he might be able to help him teach. It had been nearly ten years since he had seen John and finding him might prove to be very difficult. He had no idea as to where John had gone to teach so he would have to search the many reservations of the area. What scared him was the fact that he would have to go into these reservations and find John without drawing attention to himself. Though he knew that he would be among the Native people, the idea still frightened him.

Grandfather went back to the original reservation where he had met John. There, he hoped to find one of the students that he had taught with John. Possibly they would know where to find him. He had trouble finding the original camp area he had used. The landscape had changed so much, and now the little stream that he once camped by was nothing more than an irrigation ditch. He pushed beyond the original camp area to the thickest stand of trees he could find. It was even more dangerous to be here now since the land was cultivated and civilized. He would have to take more care than ever before to hide his camp. The fear of getting close to the reservation now was almost overwhelming to a point where he wanted to abandon his camp and go back to his people. The memories of the past pain hammered at his heart very heavily, especially being now so close to the reservation.

For the next several days, he stayed close to his camp, exploring the immediate area and hoping that someone would happen by that he could talk to. Several times he would go into the most populated parts of the reservation but only at night. He wanted to take no chances of being caught and he wanted to be assured of an easy escape if necessary. He found that the reservation now was a little more modern, but still the conditions were nothing more than slumlike. He roamed from house to house, trying to find some clue as to who were the occupants. He was hoping that there would be some evidence of one of his past students. That would be an extreme help, for he would not then be forced to go to a stranger and ask for John. His several late-night excursions into the village produced no evidence of any of his students and Grandfather began to grow very frustrated.

Early one morning, as Grandfather sat in his sacred area praying, he noticed a young woman approaching the area where he once camped long ago. With her was a very young girl, probably no older than five. He watched with great interest as the woman approached his old camp and sat down by the irrigation ditch with the child. He watched in fascination as the young woman lifted her hands in prayer and then spread some herbs around Grandfather's old camp area. Grandfather's heart soared as he watched her. There had been several young girls that John had brought to Grandfather many years ago, and possibly this could be one of them. Without hesitation and with his heart filled with anticipation he began to move closer to the young woman. As soon as he reached the clearing, she turned, saw Grandfather, and immediately ran to him. She gave him a warm hug and said, "I knew you'd come back, I knew you would come."

Grandfather began to feel the tears welling up in his eyes. This had been one of the young girls he had taught years ago. She was here practicing the old ways and teaching her daughter to pray in the old way. It was obvious to Grandfather now that this young woman had probably come to this place many times before, hoping to find him. His heart soared, for now he was witnessing his teachings become reality. He and the young woman sat by the ditch and talked for hours. Grandfather's heart began to sink as she told of all the past years. There had been so much pain and ridicule. Conditions remained much the same as they were, and people seemed even more broken, especially the old ones. She told Grandfather that she was the only one left in the village from the ones Grandfather had long ago taught.

She told Grandfather that she was the only one who had practiced what he had taught her. She drew a lot of ridicule for doing so, even from some of those who Grandfather had taught. She then had to practice her skills in secret, but even then, people still taunted her. It was only in the past few months that she could practice in the open. Now she was passing the skills down to her daughter. It seemed that many in the tribe were beginning to worship in the open again. She then went on to tell Grandfather about John. John had gone to the reservation of the north to try to teach the children. He was a schoolteacher anyway, so he thought that he could add the old skills to what he taught in the schools. However, she had not heard from him in many years and did not know if he was still in the same place.

Leaving his camp area the next day, Grandfather headed north to the reservation where John was last known to be. Grandfather began to grow excited as he approached the northern reservation. He had seen what his teaching had done for the woman, now he hoped that it would even do more for John. Possibly John had been successful with teaching the old ways to the children. After all, the woman was now teaching her child. But Grandfather's hopes were dashed when he finally got to the reservation. As he searched the village through the night he could find no evidence of John. He pushed the light of dawn as far as he could and had to abandon his search for the day. He would return again the next night, in hopes of finding anything that would give him any clue as to John's home.

Grandfather searched the village every night for the next several days, but found nothing that would lead to John. He then began to visit the village during the day, but staying to cover so as not to be seen. He watched the people of the village going and coming for several days, but there was no sight of John. Grandfather now feared that John was no longer with the village. In a last-ditch attempt to find John, he went to the outskirts of the local school and watched the children and teachers come and go. John was not seen at all. It was obvious to Grandfather that John had moved on, but had no idea as to where, or even how to begin to look. It was then that Grandfather heard a distant familiar sound—the sound of stone hitting stone—the music of the old skills.

Moving in the brush along the outskirts of the schoolyard, Grandfather began to stalk in the direction of the sound. Within a few minutes he entered a small secluded clearing where a young boy sat with his back toward Grandfather. The boy was chipping at a rock, obviously trying to make an arrow point. Grandfather deftly walked behind the boy and put his hand on his shoulder. The boy jumped up with a start and bolted to the other side of the clearing. He looked at Grandfather in utter amazement and fear. Grandfather smiled at him and the boy seemed to relax, but quickly put the stones he was working on behind him. Grandfather reached out his hands and gestured to the rocks. The boy reluctantly handed Grandfather the rocks, in a sheepish manner. Grandfather looked at the stones, quickly chipped off several flakes, then handed the finished arrowhead back to the boy. He took the arrowhead and looked at it in amazement, then at Grandfather.

Feeling that he now had gained the boy's confidence, he asked him where he had learned to chip stone. The boy told Grandfather that he could not tell him. Grandfather then told the little boy that the person who taught him how to make the stones talk was probably the same person Grandfather had taught. The boy then told Grandfather that if anyone knew that he had learned from John, then he would get in trouble. As soon as he heard the name John, Grandfather's heart soared. He asked the boy again to take him to John and he reluctantly agreed. He told Grandfather that John did not live in the village, but many miles away, and alone. He said that John did not like it when the adults came around. He only liked to talk to children. The boy worried that John would be angry at him for bringing an adult.

The little boy led Grandfather along an old overgrown road and then deep into the forest. He took a maze of trails, many of them very rugged. He told Grandfather that he was sorry that it was taking them so long to get there but John had told him not to use the same trails going and coming. Grandfather knew that he had taught John the "scout ways" but he could not understand why he was using these techniques around his own home. Finally they arrived at an old shack, nestled deep in the woods. The shack was built to fit into the landscape and was rather rugged and weather tight. The area around the shack was litter free and very neat. There was no evidence of destruction to the earth, instead the surrounding vegetation was the healthiest that Grandfather had seen yet along his journey. It became plainly obvious that this was John's house. Grandfather's heart soared, realizing that John was still living in perfect balance with the earth.

The young boy told Grandfather to stay where he was while he went to speak to John and find out if he would see Grandfather. As the boy entered the clearing a voice called out from the house, telling the boy to come in. The young boy looked amazed at John's ability to know he was there. Grandfather watched the boy go to the front door. There in the door stood a man talking to him, but Grandfather was still too far away to identify him as John. The man looked angry at the boy at first and Grandfather could see him shaking his head in disapproval. Finally, the boy pulled the stone arrowhead from his pocket and the man ran from the door and in Grandfather's direction. As the man drew closer Grandfather could plainly see that it was John, and he stood up and away from the bush where he hid.

John began to hug Grandfather, even before he stopped running, and they both tumbled to the ground laughing. The young boy, who had followed John on his headlong run, stood by very confused. He had never seen John welcome anyone like this, especially an adult. He also had not seen John so happy. Without hesitation, seeing the boy's confused expression, John introduced Grandfather as the man who taught him his skills, the same skills that John had taught to the boy. Realizing that this was the old man that John had spoken about for years, the boy ran up and gave Grandfather a big hug. Grandfather could plainly see that the little boy now held him in awe, but could not understand why. John told Grandfather that he was a legend around here and that many people had more than once heard the story.

Grandfather then asked John where all his students were, and John pointed to the young boy, sadly. As they spent the day together, John told Grandfather the horrors of his life. Many years ago, just a few weeks after he had left Grandfather, John had gone to a white man's school to get a job as a teacher. Most of the children in the school were Native American so John thought that he would stand a good chance of being able to teach some of the old skills. He was hired for that coming year and would be teaching a history class for the fourth grade. It would have been perfect because the subject that he had to teach was early American history and he could easily work in the skills. Shortly after beginning to teach, he found that most of the history books and literature were very prejudiced against the Native American, leaning toward the white interpretation. He began to teach his children, not from the books but from that which he knew to be the truth.

Within the first month of teaching he was reprimanded severely by the administration for veering off the class outlines, and for teaching lies. Within the second month, he was reprimanded twice more, then fired when he was caught teaching the class the tribal religion. From that point, he tried wandering and teaching, but to no avail and at best with very limited success. He had been effectively banned from teaching in the white man's school system and now had no way of passing down his knowledge. In fact, he had been put under investigation for teaching communism, as the white man called it. People of the tribe began to avoid him because of fear that they would be linked with his teaching. He finally had no other choice than to move away from the tribe and try to teach anyone who would come along. In the past years, he only had two students, one of whom was the young boy who brought Grandfather to him.

Grandfather's hopes were dashed once again. It was not because the children did not want to learn, for they seemed to have a passion for the old ways. It was the white man again who forced their ways and opinions on the people. John told Grandfather that in the past he would get several kids together to teach, but within a short time outside pressures or ridicule would eventually drive them away. John said, however, that he was not giving up hope because many of the people were again seeking the ancient knowledge. He believed that one day, maybe not in his life, but in the distant future, people would seek these ways again. He was beginning to see a change in the determination of the tribe for freedom to do and act as they pleased, free from the white man's scorn.

Grandfather stayed with John and the young boy for several days, learning all he could about John's attempts to teach. Finally, with no hope left in his heart, he left John. He felt sorry for the way John had to live and what he had to give up to practice the old ways. Grandfather felt so responsible for getting John involved with his dream, his vision. If it were not for Grandfather's influence, John might be a good teacher today in some school where he might do some good. Instead, Grandfather's teaching had sentenced him to a life of ridicule. Embittered by it all, Grandfather did nothing but wander for the next several months. Though he avoided all human contact, the spirit within was constantly directing him to find someone to teach.

Not being able to take the spiritual torment any longer, Grandfather again began to wander with a purpose. He visited any area he could where he could find children to teach. No sooner did he find someone to teach than that person was forbidden to talk to Grandfather. After many months of failure, Grandfather was beginning to feel like a disease. No one seemed to want to learn or stay with him for any time. There was always something more important going on in the white man's world that would ultimately drive them away. The frustration grew daily, yet the spirit to teach someone, anyone, still remained within him. Finally, being able to take no more pain, he decided to head back to his people and live out his remaining years. His vision, as far as he was concerned, was dead. He was too old to go on.

During his long journey back to his people, Grandfather grew very suicidal. He could not accept the fact that he had given his entire life to the preservation of the old ways, and was now realizing that his life's work would be for nothing. Though he would not have lived his life any other way, he felt that he was not worthy of the vision to teach, for he had failed so miserably. He would head back to his people and live out his last remaining years among close friends and family. As far as he was concerned, there was nothing else he could do, nothing else he could learn. The driving voice within had become a dying murmur, and now the entire spirit world had seemed to abandon him. After all, if he was not living his vision, then he was of no use to the spirit world.

He finally reached his people and asked for a council, before he would camp within the perimeter of the village. One night, nearly a full moon after he made camp, the village asked him to come to council. Grandfather told the council of his failure, that his vision no longer lived, and that he did not feel worthy to live within the village. He felt a little strange approaching the council, for he was one of the oldest to attend. Now nearing eighty-one winters of age there were but two older than he. After Grandfather told of his wanderings and many failures, one of the two elders told Grandfather that his vision was not over. He suggested to Grandfather that he take a vision quest to clarify his path.

He urged Grandfather to understand that a vision was not over until a person took the final walk to the Creator.

Grandfather reluctantly accepted the elder's advice, but did not quest. He could see no good that could come of it. Instead, he lived within the village and tried to make peace with himself in his final days. For the better part of the year, Grandfather did nothing but survive. Each day he was tormented by the words of the elder but would not give in to the quest. Finally there came the day when one of the last elders of the tribe died, and soon to follow was the elder who had given Grandfather the advice to quest. As he lay dying, he asked Grandfather once again to quest, which was the last request and the last words he spoke. There was such an urgency in his voice that Grandfather had no choice but to quest the next day, if for no other reason than to honor the old one's spirit.

Before first light, Grandfather wandered far out into the wilderness to vision quest. He had to honor the spirit of the old one but he also realized that he was the elder now. He would have to lead the people; after all, the next in line was ten years his junior. He began to convince himself that his people now needed his wisdom and it might be possible that this was why he had been met with so many failures. Maybe it was his destiny to lead his people rather than to teach. It was these and many other questions that followed Grandfather into this vision quest that day. As he sat down in the quest area, he felt a strange sensation. It had been many months since he had given himself over to the quest, but it was more than that. No sooner had he sat down than the warrior spirit of his youth returned. It pointed demandingly to the east, where a young white coyote howled, then pawed at ancient stones by the stream bank. Grandfather knew without a doubt that he would go east now and find the white coyote.

Whether by plan or design, I was on that riverbank when I saw Grandfather. The coyote howled and tears came to Grandfather's eyes. Today his vision lives, beyond even my wildest dreams. Though many times I feel unworthy and am constantly beaten by my own flesh, the quest to teach remains on fire deep within me. I am driven by the same fire that drove Grandfather. I have hope, the same hope that he placed within my soul so many years ago. The fire still burns, and now many have the fire. Grandfather was right. Someday people will seek again the old ways, the only truth.

These stories were very important to me. They were not only teaching devices, they were a spark to send me to these places, and I hope those who read this book will search out the truths. To give instruction would satisfy the needs of most people, but that is not my goal. My goal is to give the reader a picture of the world we live in, the forgotten world. This book explains that it is not easily come by and a search for the truths must occur before knowledge is attained. Grandfather's life was full of every emotion, every feeling, and they did not come from listening to his elders. He had to seek them out for himself as I wish the reader to do. I am a "coyote teacher."

If you would like to go further and discover more about the wilderness with Tom Brown, please write for information to:

> The Tracker
> Tom Brown, Tracker, Inc.
> P.O. Box 173
> Asbury, N.J. 08802-0173
> (908) 479-4681
> Tracking, Nature, Wilderness
>   Survival School
>
> www.trackerschool.com